Dublin Daze

by
TOM CASSIDY

Cassidy
COMICS

First published 2014

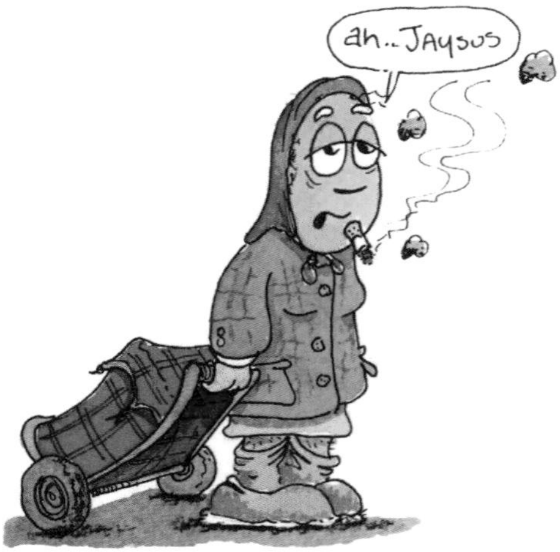
ah.. JAYSUS

www.cassidycomics.com

ISBN 9781499181739

FOR ME MAMMY.
GEORGINA.
WHO ONLY CRACKED
ONCE IN THE HEAT
OF BATTLE....

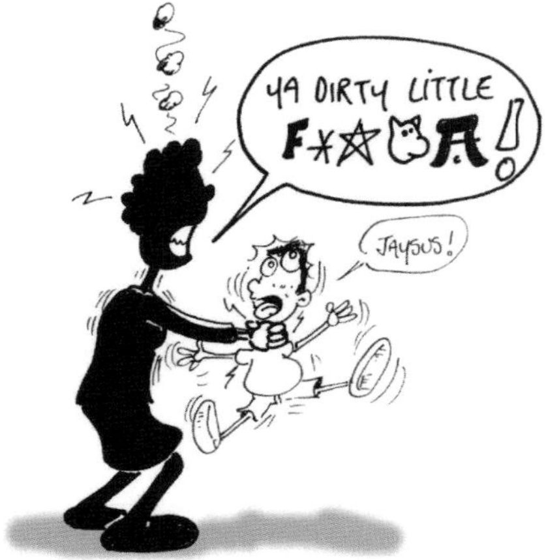
YA DIRTY LITTLE
JAYSUS!

Dublin Daze was brought to life by the author's lifelong fascination with Dublin's Northside and its inhabitants. From its crumbling buildings to its windswept diverse cross section of characters, from inner city to outer Pale and the lands beyond the Avoca Café on the N7.

It's mission is to keep you focused on enjoying those funny little moments we all witness along the way before they melt away into the nothingness of our own rotten decomposing grey matter.

HAVE FUN
Cassidy

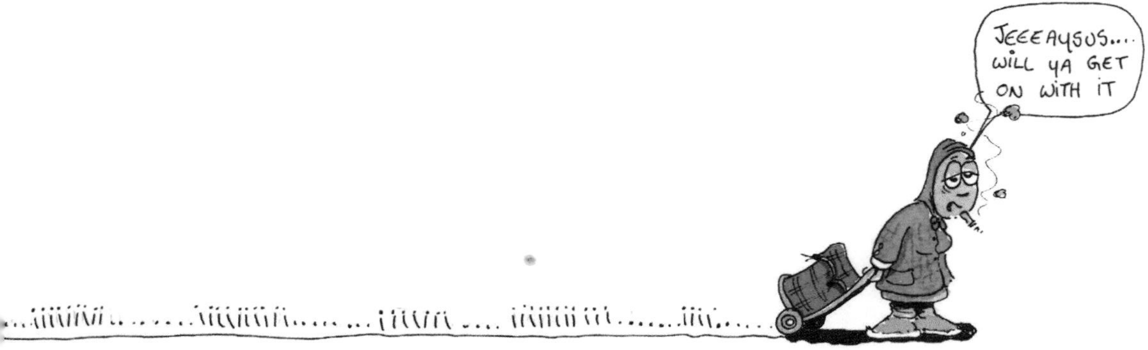
JEEEAYSUS.....
WILL YA GET
ON WITH IT

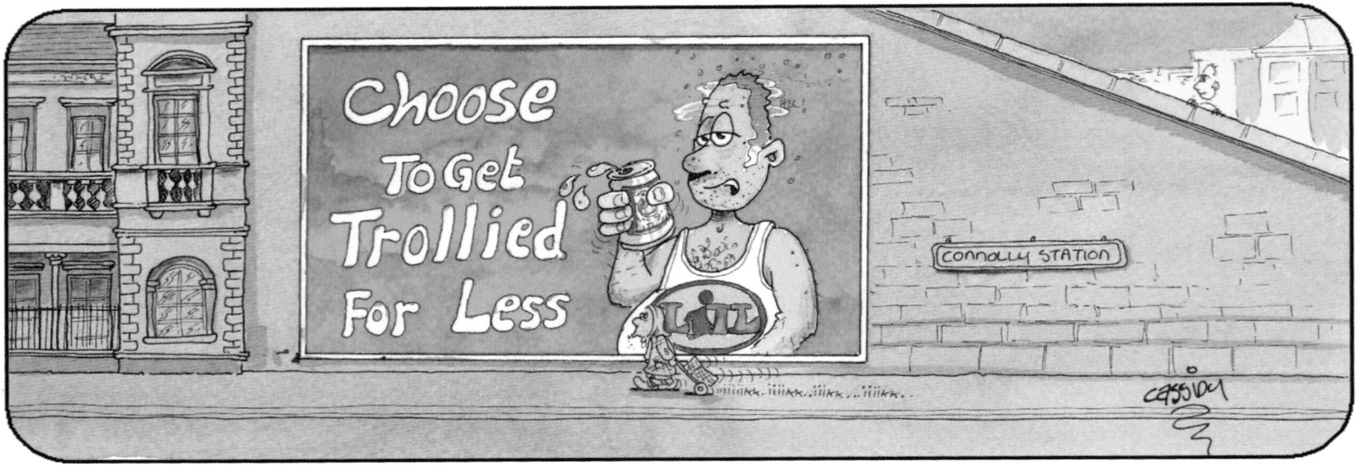
Choose To Get Trollied For Less
HIC!
LiTL
CONNOLLY STATION
iiiiikk..iiiikk..iiikk...iiiikk..
CASSIDY

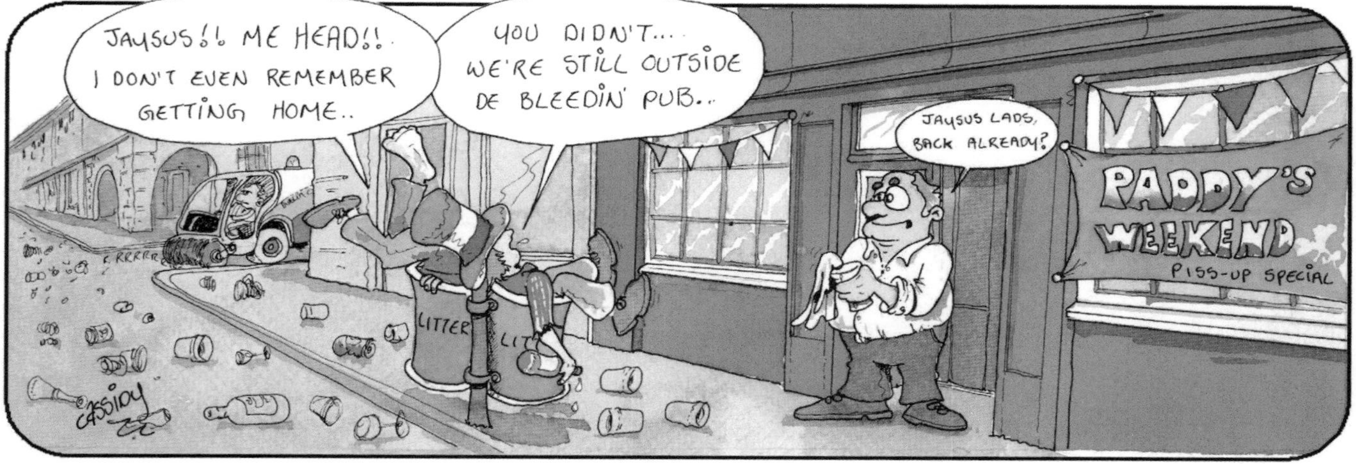
JAYSUS!! ME HEAD!!
I DON'T EVEN REMEMBER GETTING HOME..
YOU DIDN'T....
WE'RE STILL OUTSIDE DE BLEEDIN' PUB...
JAYSUS LADS, BACK ALREADY?
PADDY'S WEEKEND
PISS-UP SPECIAL
LITTER
CASSIDY

CROUCH...
...TOUCH..
...PAUSE...
...ENGAGE!
LET ME GUESS....
RUGBY SEASON'S STARTED
ching..

Dublin Daze

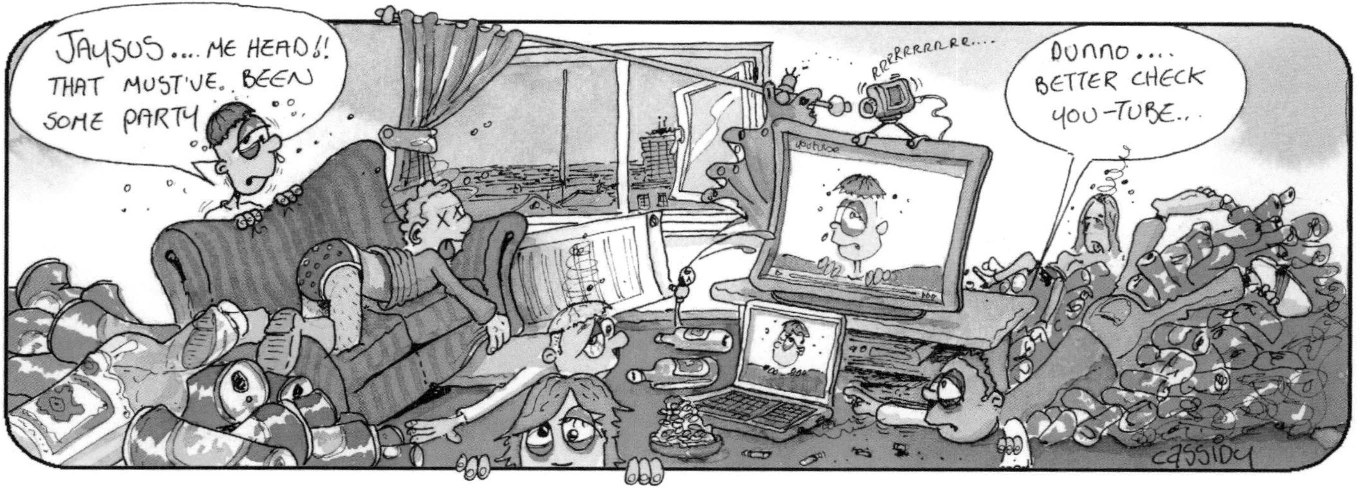
JAYSUS.... ME HEAD!! THAT MUST'VE BEEN SOME PARTY
RRRRRRRRRR....
DUNNO.... BETTER CHECK YOU-TUBE..
CASSIDY

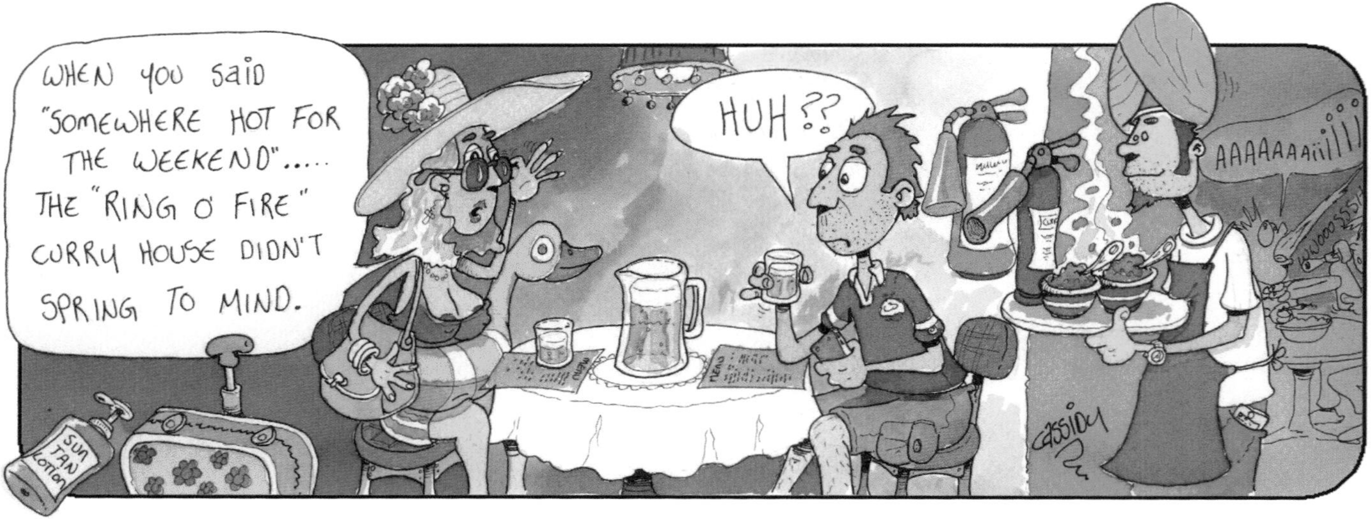
WHEN YOU SAID "SOMEWHERE HOT FOR THE WEEKEND"..... THE "RING O' FIRE" CURRY HOUSE DIDN'T SPRING TO MIND.
HUH ??
SUN TAN LOTION
CASSIDY

Dublin Daze

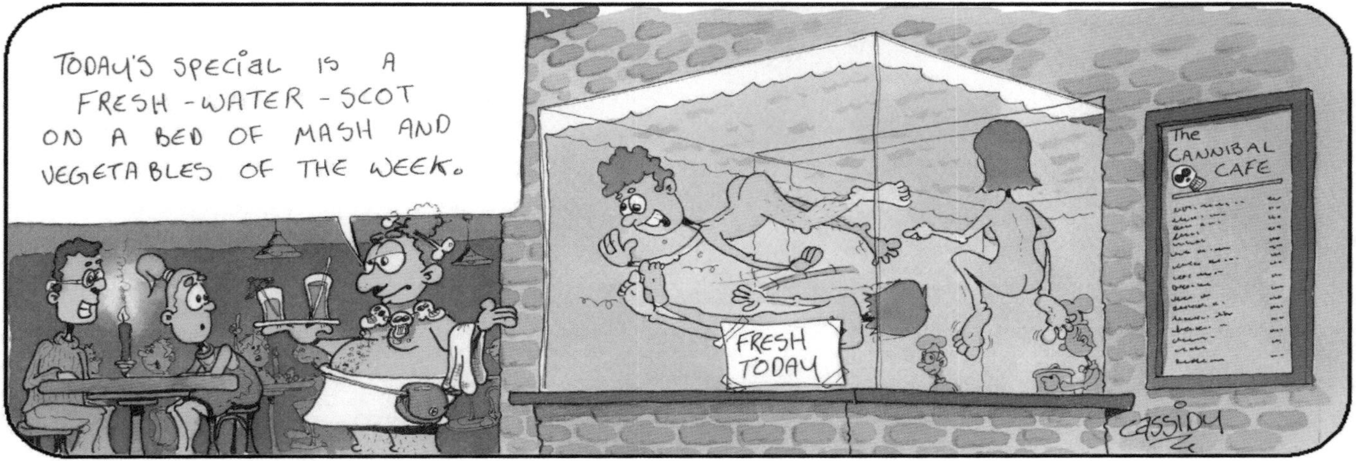
TODAY'S SPECIAL IS A FRESH-WATER-SCOT ON A BED OF MASH AND VEGETABLES OF THE WEEK.
FRESH TODAY
The CANNIBAL CAFE
CASSIDY

'EEEERE FRED, I'M WATCHIN' THE SIMPSONS ..... I COULDN'T GIVE A CRAP WHAT THE HOMERPHOBICS SAY
I THOUGHT UR NAME WAS FRED
IT'S 'HOMO'
CASSIDY

Dublin Daze

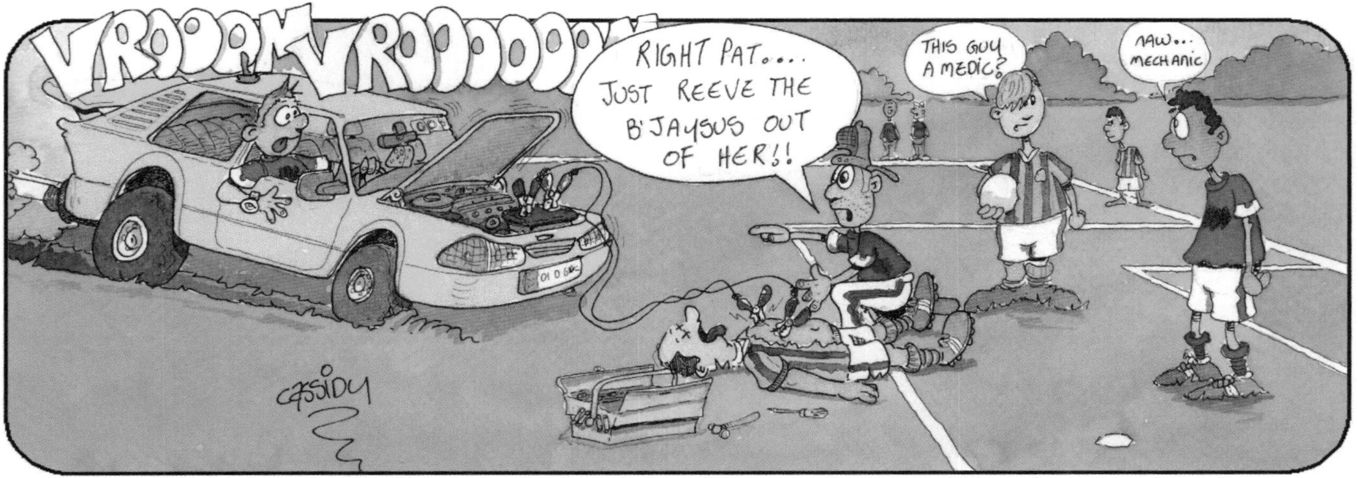
VROOOM VROOOOOOOM
RIGHT PAT.... JUST REEVE THE B'JAYSUS OUT OF HER!!
THIS GUY A MEDIC?
NAW... MECHANIC
CASSIDY

DADDY??
I'M AFRAID IT LOOKS LIKE A BLOWN HEAD GASKET...
blub... blub... blub
cassidy

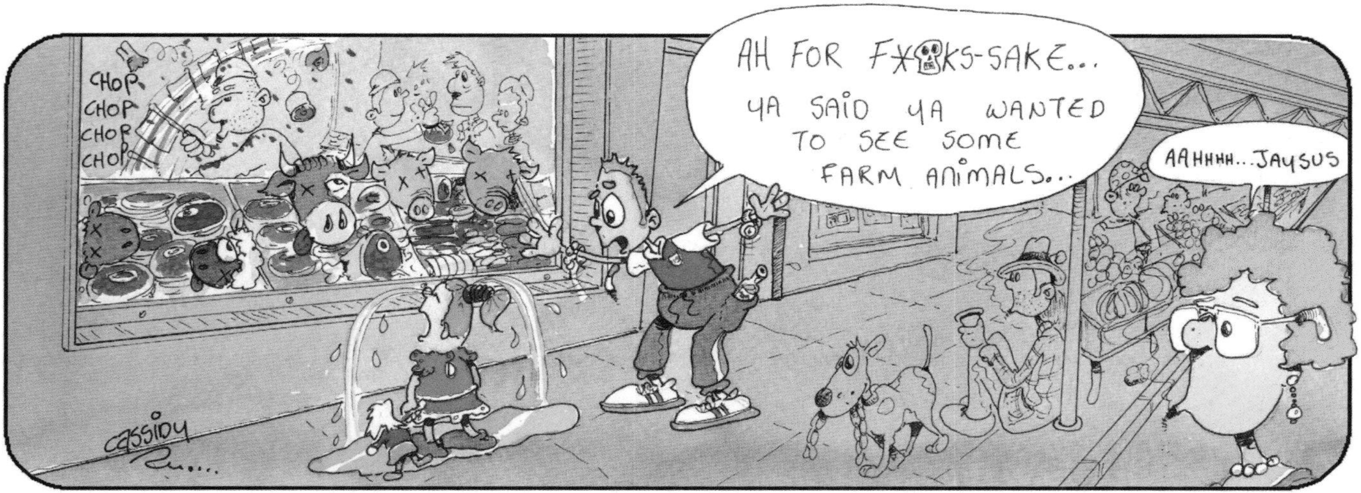
CHOP
CHOP
CHOP
CHOP
AH FOR F✱☠KS-SAKE...
YA SAID YA WANTED TO SEE SOME FARM ANIMALS...
AAHHHH...JAYSUS
CASSIDY

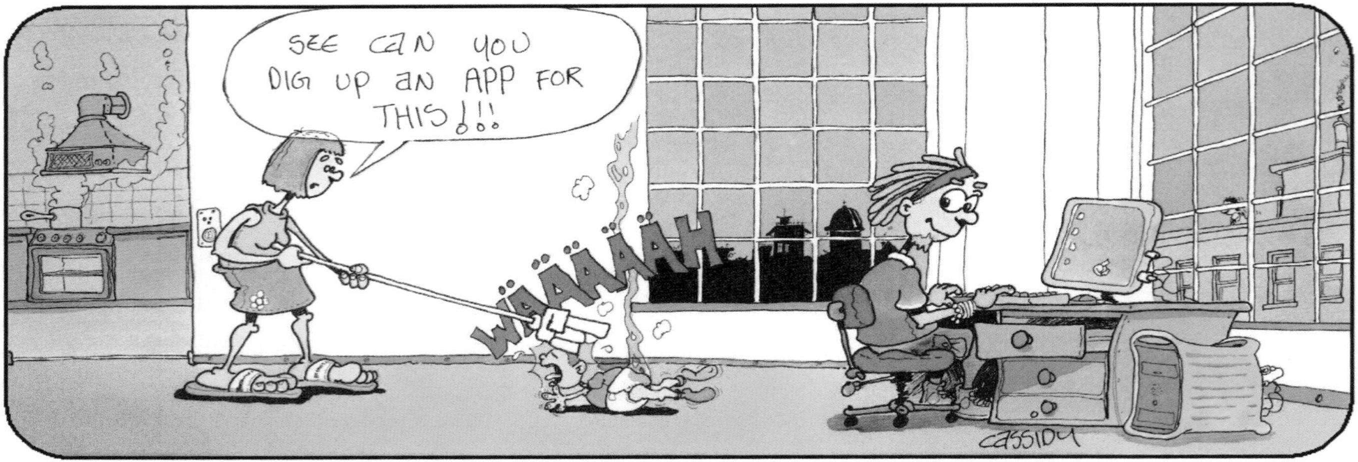
SEE CAN YOU DIG UP AN APP FOR THIS¡!!
WÄÄÄÄÄÄH
CASSIDY

Dublin Daze

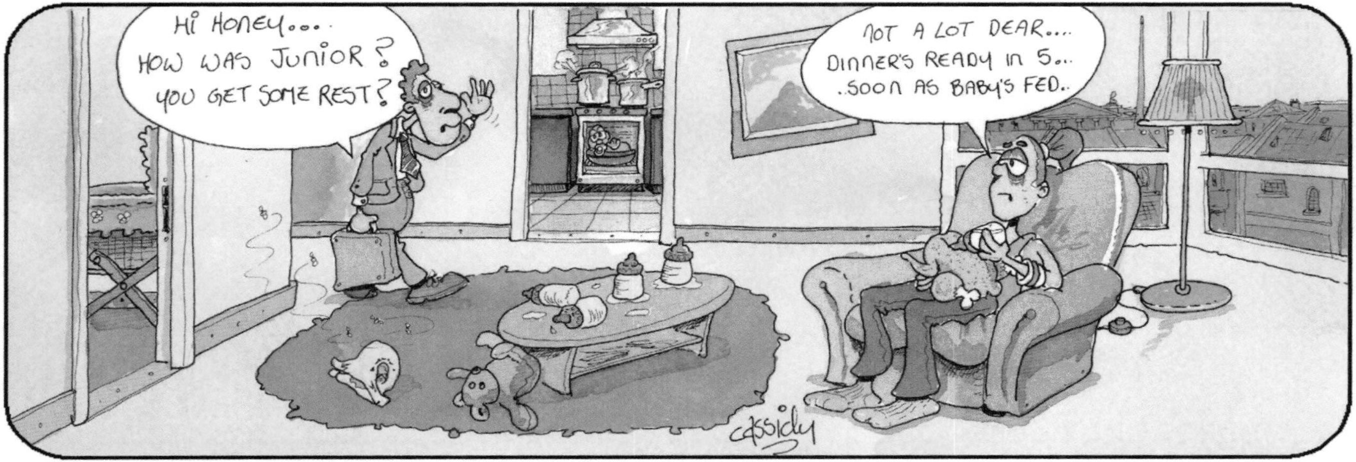
HI HONEY....
HOW WAS JUNIOR?
YOU GET SOME REST?
NOT A LOT DEAR....
DINNER'S READY IN 5...
..SOON AS BABY'S FED..
cassidy

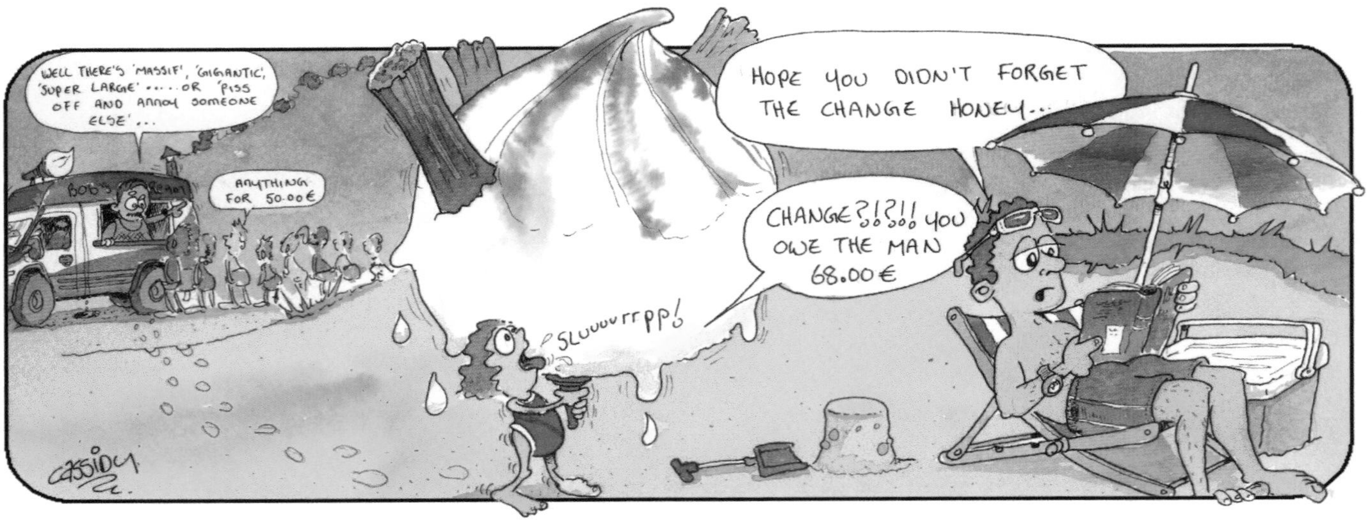
WELL THERE'S 'MASSIF', 'GIGANTIC', 'SUPER LARGE' .....OR 'PISS OFF AND ANNOY SOMEONE ELSE'...
ANYTHING FOR 50.00€
HOPE YOU DIDN'T FORGET THE CHANGE HONEY...
CHANGE?!?!! YOU OWE THE MAN 68.00€
SLUUUURRPP!
CASSIDY

Dublin Daze

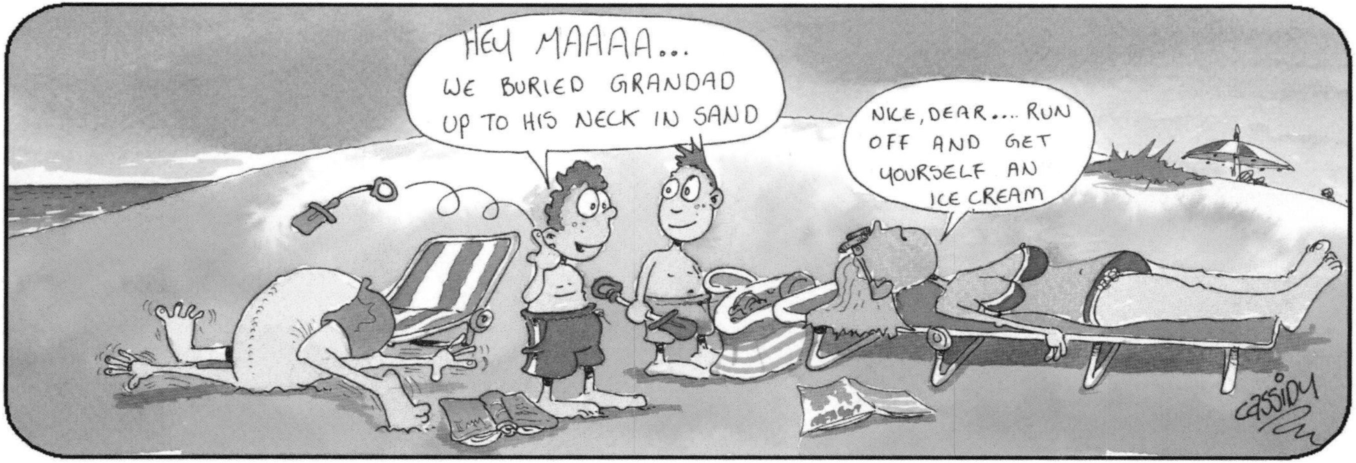
HEY MAAAA...
WE BURIED GRANDAD
UP TO HIS NECK IN SAND
NICE, DEAR.... RUN
OFF AND GET
YOURSELF AN
ICE CREAM
CASSIDY

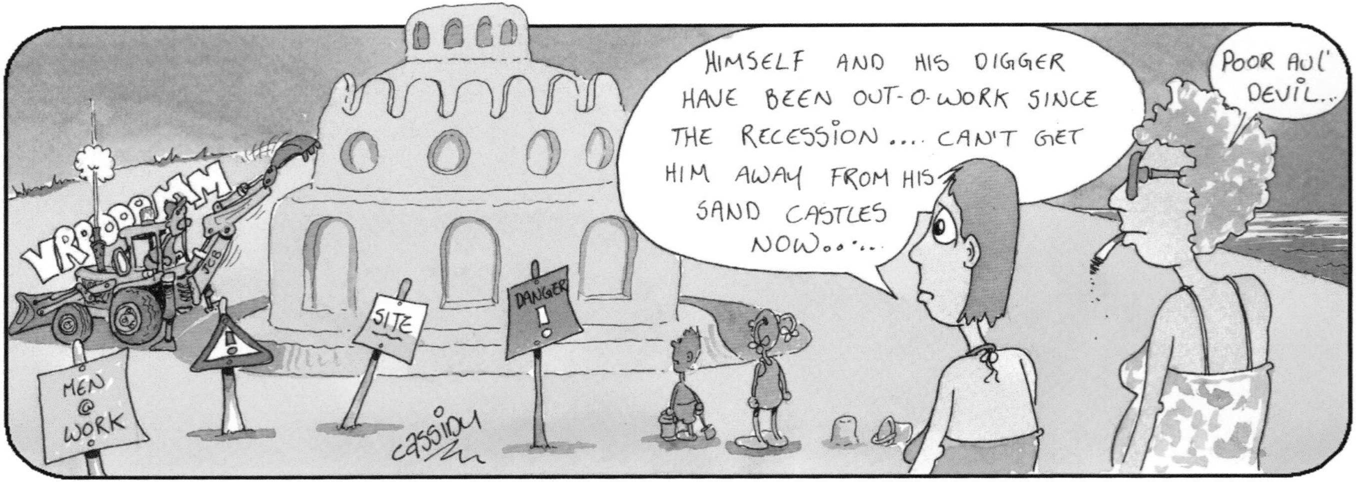
HIMSELF AND HIS DIGGER HAVE BEEN OUT-O-WORK SINCE THE RECESSION.... CAN'T GET HIM AWAY FROM HIS SAND CASTLES NOW.....
POOR AUL' DEVIL...
MEN @ WORK
SITE
DANGER !
JCB
CASSIDY

Dublin Daze

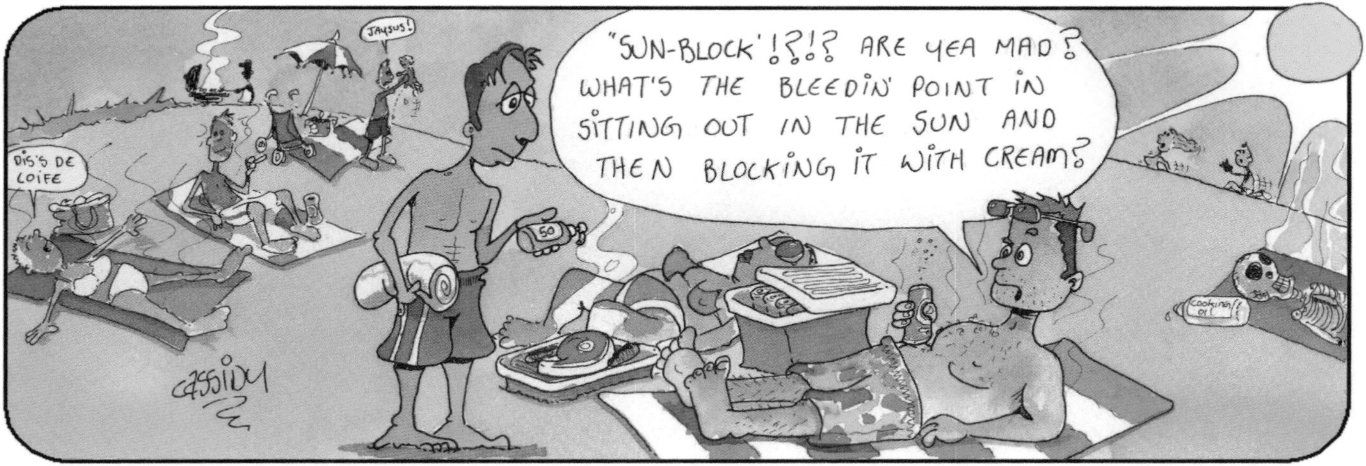
"SUN-BLOCK'!?!? ARE YEA MAD? WHAT'S THE BLEEDIN' POINT IN SITTING OUT IN THE SUN AND THEN BLOCKING IT WITH CREAM?
DIS'S DE LOIFE
JAYSUS!
50
COOKING OIL
CASSIDY

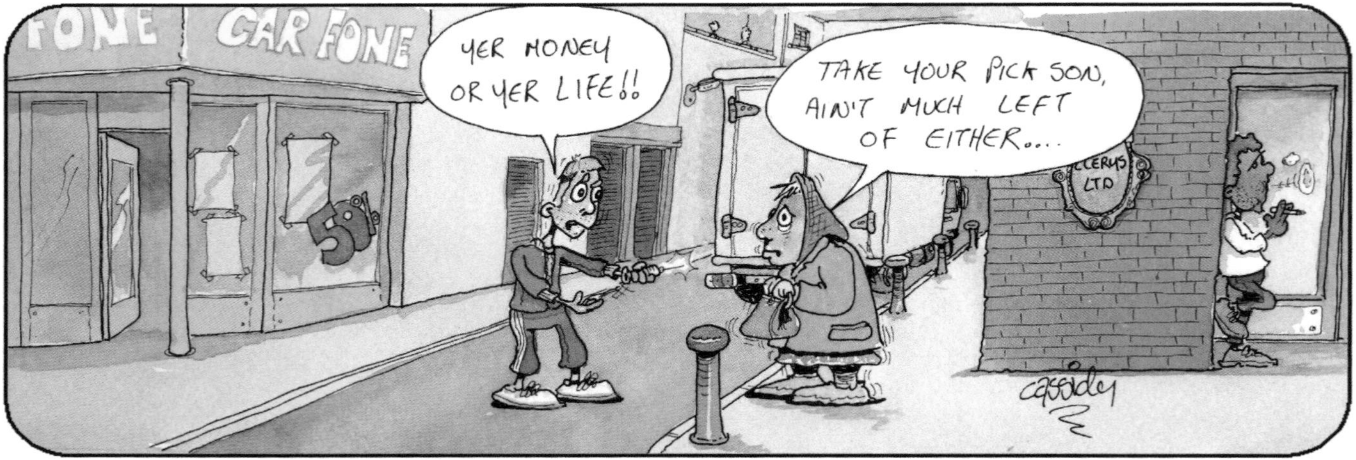
FONE
CAR FONE
YER MONEY OR YER LIFE!!
TAKE YOUR PICK SON, AIN'T MUCH LEFT OF EITHER...
CLERYS LTD
cassidy

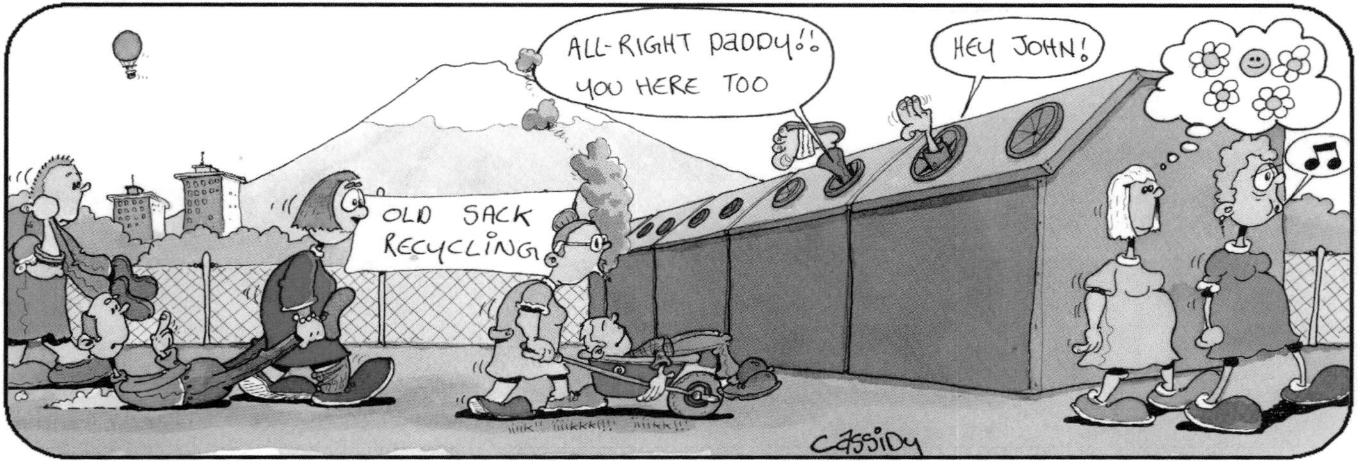
OLD SACK
RECYCLING
ALL-RIGHT PADDY!!
YOU HERE TOO
HEY JOHN!
CASSIDY

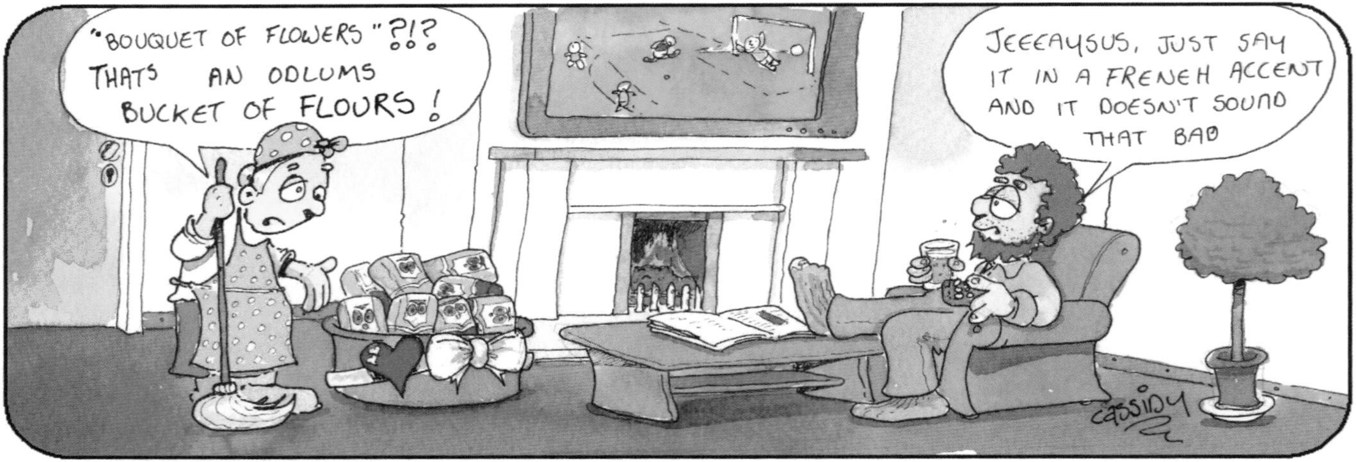
"BOUQUET OF FLOWERS"?!? THATS AN ODLUMS BUCKET OF FLOURS!
JEEEAYSUS, JUST SAY IT IN A FRENCH ACCENT AND IT DOESN'T SOUND THAT BAD
CASSIDY

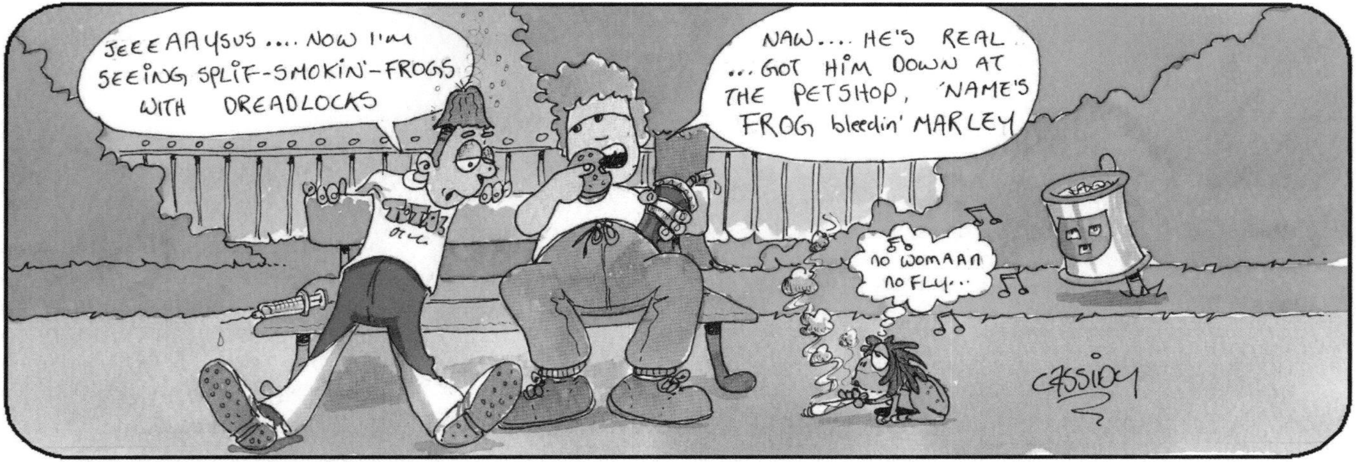
JEEEAAYSUS .... NOW I'M SEEING SPLIF-SMOKIN'-FROGS WITH DREADLOCKS
NAW.... HE'S REAL ...GOT HIM DOWN AT THE PETSHOP, 'NAME'S FROG bleedin' MARLEY
no WOMAAAN no FLY...
CASSIDY

THERE MUST BE SOME SORT OF RELIGIOUS ANGLE TO THIS TAX SYSTEM.... WE'RE ALL BEING CRUCIFIED
ZZZZZZZ
GOVERNMENT BUILDINGS
NO SCUM LOITERING
HELP
HOME OWNER
MORTGAGE ARREARS
OWNED BY BANK
OWNED BY GERMANY
I'M WITH STUPID
KLINK
KLINK
CASSIDY

Dublin Daze

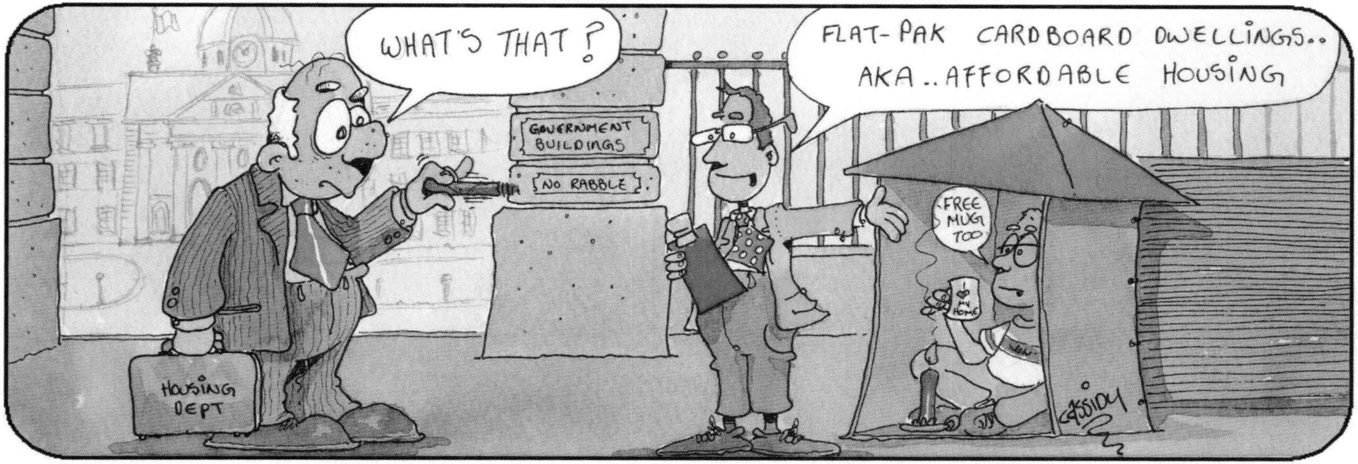
WHAT'S THAT ?
FLAT-PAK CARDBOARD DWELLINGS..
AKA..AFFORDABLE HOUSING
GOVERNMENT BUILDINGS
NO RABBLE
FREE MUG TOO
HOUSING DEPT
CASSIDY

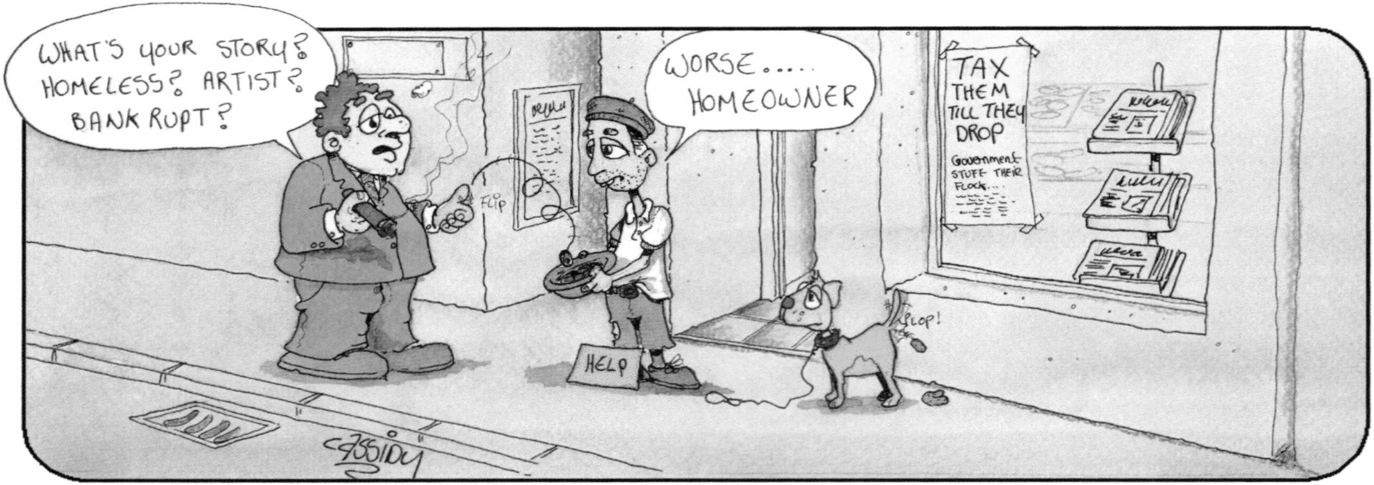
WHAT'S YOUR STORY? HOMELESS? ARTIST? BANK RUPT?
WORSE..... HOMEOWNER
TAX THEM TILL THEY DROP
Government STUFF THEIR FLOCK....
FLIP
HELP
PLOP!
CASSIDY

Dublin Daze

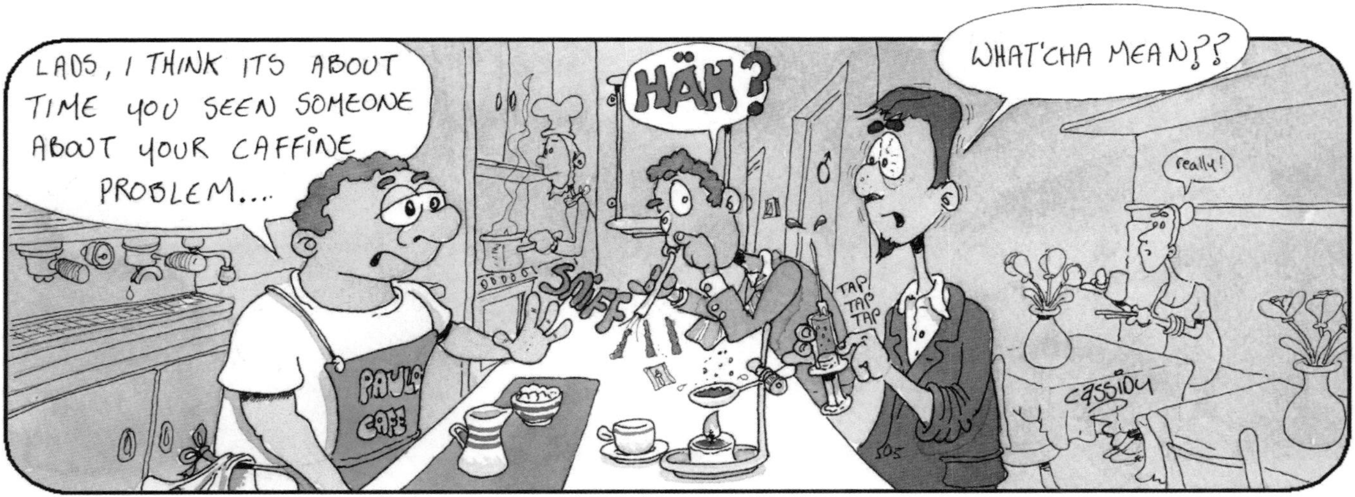
LADS, I THINK ITS ABOUT TIME YOU SEEN SOMEONE ABOUT YOUR CAFFINE PROBLEM....
HÄH?
WHAT'CHA MEAN?¿
really!
SNIFF
TAP TAP TAP
PAULO CAFE
CASSIDY

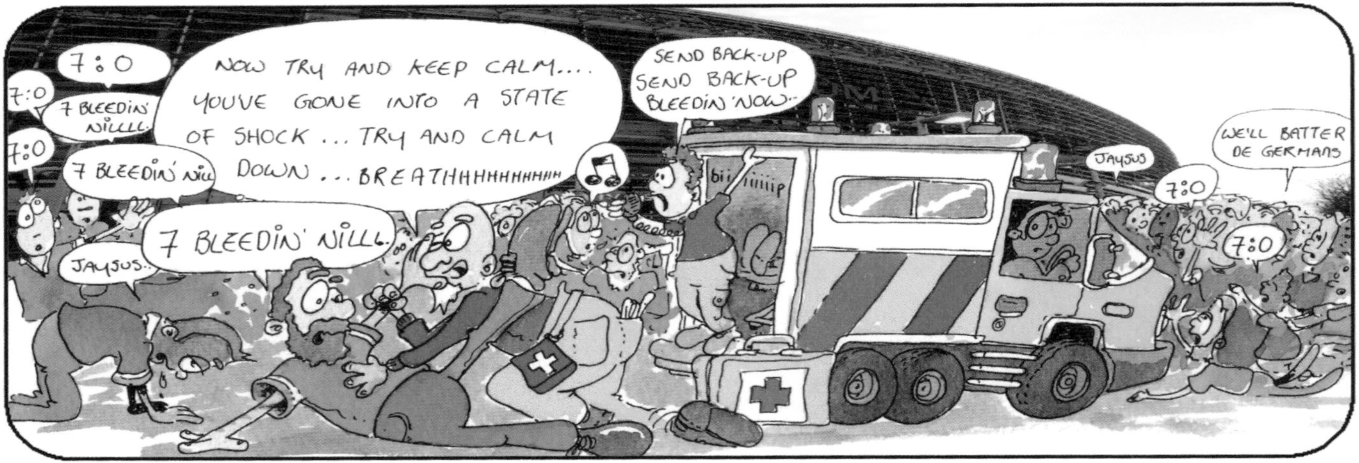
7:0
7:0
7 BLEEDIN' NILLLL.
7:0
7 BLEEDIN' NILL
NOW TRY AND KEEP CALM.... YOU'VE GONE INTO A STATE OF SHOCK ... TRY AND CALM DOWN ... BREATHHHHHHHHHH
7 BLEEDIN' NILLL.
JAYSUS..
SEND BACK-UP SEND BACK-UP BLEEDIN' NOW..
biiiiiiip
JAYSUS
7:0
WE'LL BATTER DE GERMANS
7:0

Dublin Daze

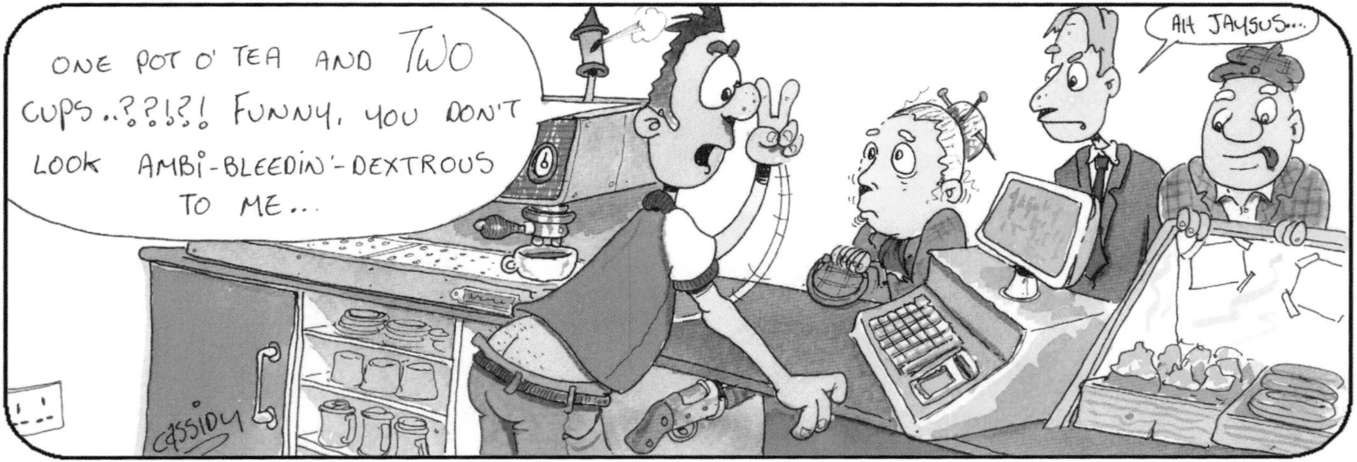
ONE POT O' TEA AND TWO CUPS..??!?! FUNNY, YOU DON'T LOOK AMBI-BLEEDIN'-DEXTROUS TO ME...
AH JAYSUS...
CASSIDY

.... AND I DECIDED TO STOP HOARDING MONEY AND LIVE 'THE LIFE' BEFORE I DIED .... BUT THEN I DIDN'T...
...DIDN'T TREAT YOURSELF?
NO.... HE DIDN'T DIE.
BUMMER...
ANY CHANCE OF A BIT OF CUNÁS
DUBLIN CITY
CASSIDY

Dublin Daze

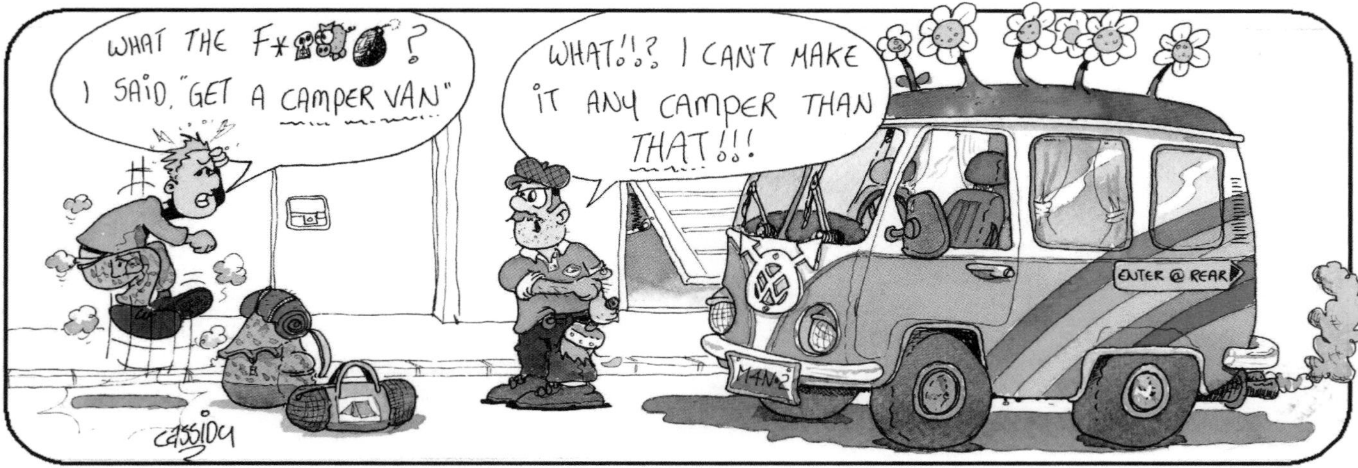
WHAT THE F*? I SAID, "GET A CAMPER VAN"
WHAT!!? I CAN'T MAKE IT ANY CAMPER THAN THAT!!!
ENTER @ REAR
M4N-2
CASSIDY

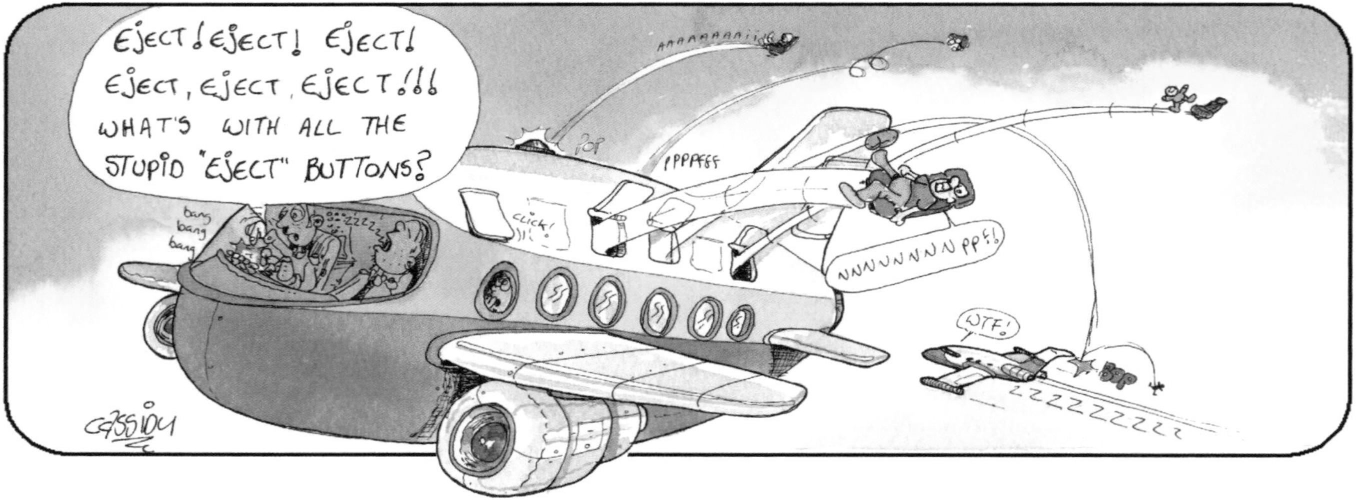
EJECT! EJECT! EJECT!
EJECT, EJECT, EJECT!!!
WHAT'S WITH ALL THE
STUPID "EJECT" BUTTONS?
bang
bang
bang
ZZZZZ
CLICK!
POP
PPPPFFF
NNNUNNNNPPF!
WTF!
ZZZZZZZZZ

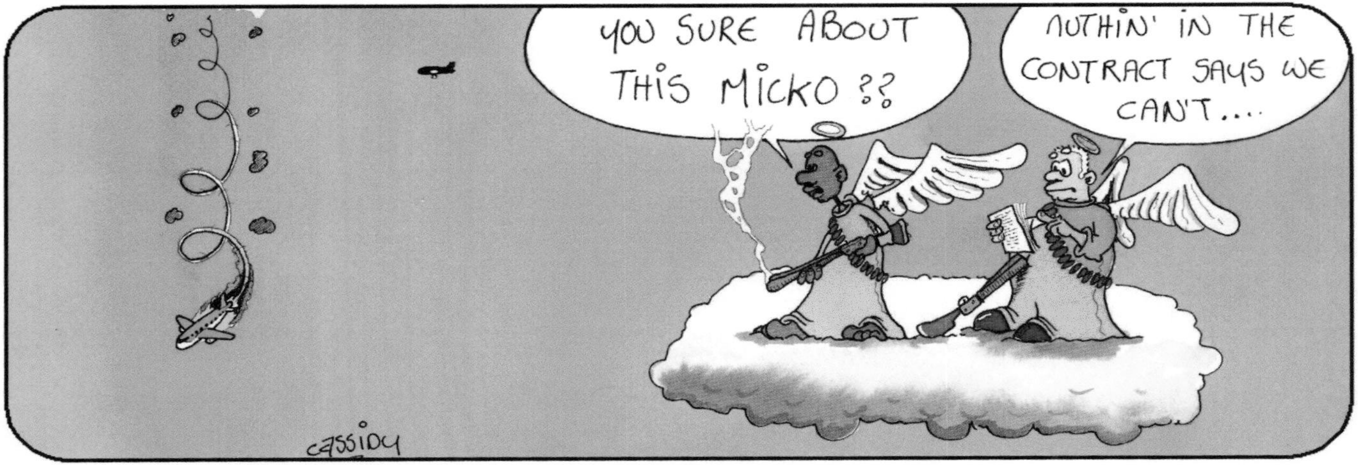
YOU SURE ABOUT THIS MICKO ??
NUTHIN' IN THE CONTRACT SAYS WE CAN'T....
CASSIDY

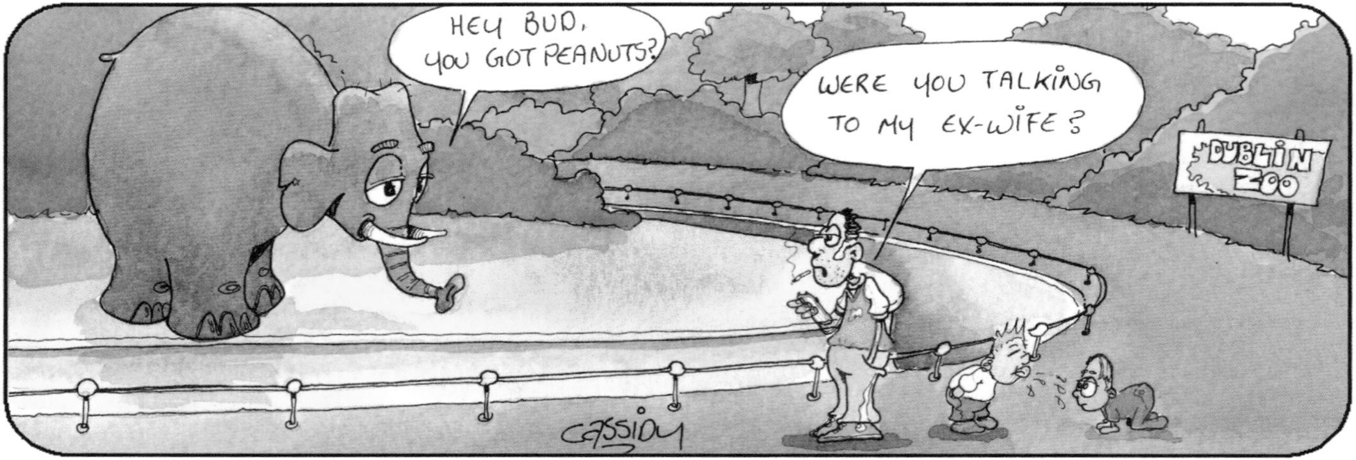
HEY BUD, YOU GOT PEANUTS?
WERE YOU TALKING TO MY EX-WIFE?
DUBLIN ZOO
CASSIDY

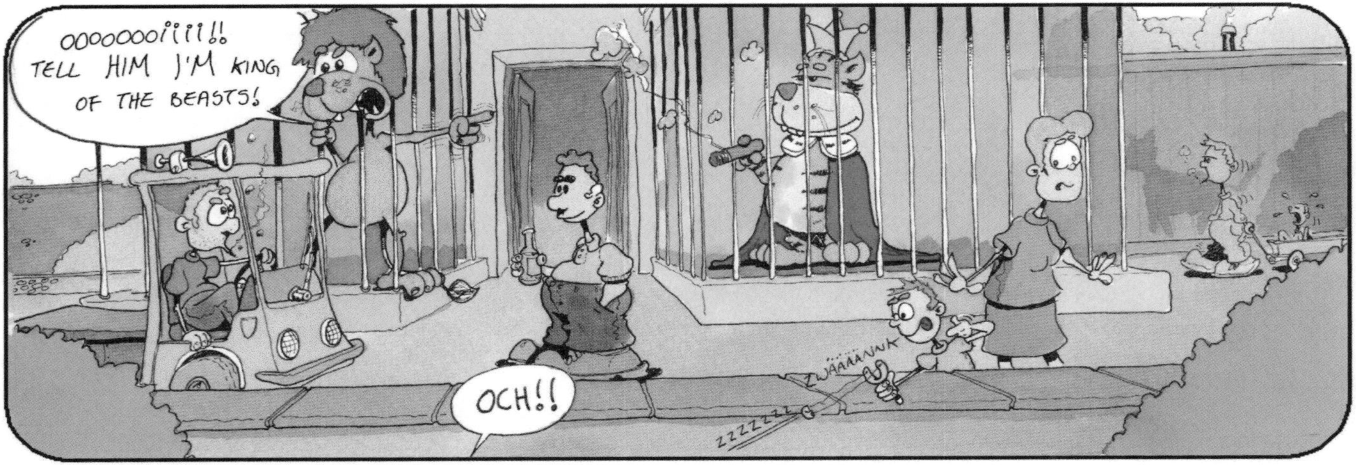
OOOOOOOOiiii!!
TELL HIM I'M KING OF THE BEASTS!
OCH!!
ZWAAAANNK
ZZZZZZZZ

WHAT'S ALL THIS?
FLYWEIGHT..
CASIO

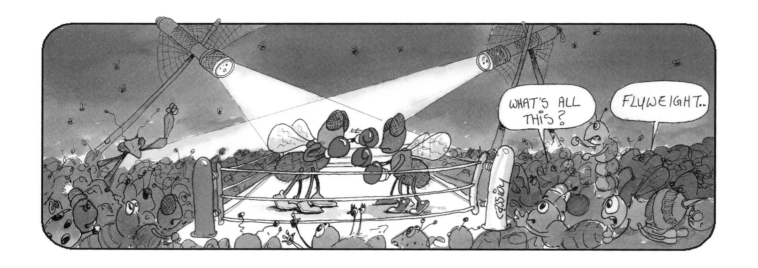

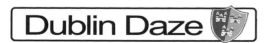

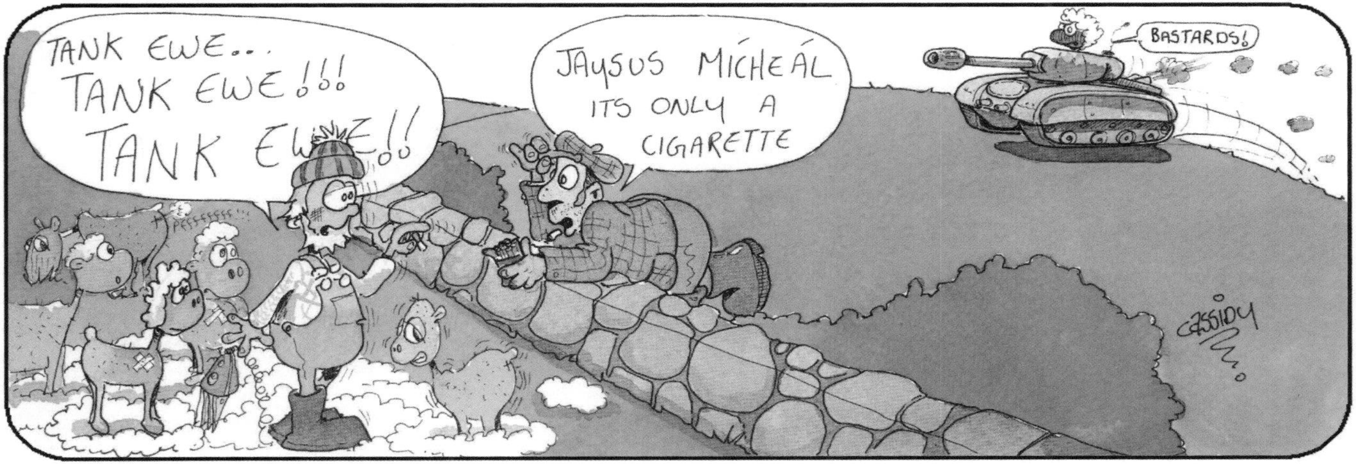
TANK EWE...
TANK EWE!!!
TANK EWE!!
JAYSUS MICHEÁL ITS ONLY A CIGARETTE
BASTARDS!
CASSIDY

RRRRRRRRRRR
iiiiiiiiiii
RRRRRR
CHUNK
RRRRR
GRIND
RRRR
EASTMEAT
QUALITY BEEF DISTRIBUTORS
DAF
WHO'S A STUPID COW NOW!!!
WAH HA HA HA...
gulp!
ZZZZZ
CASSIDY

Dublin Daze

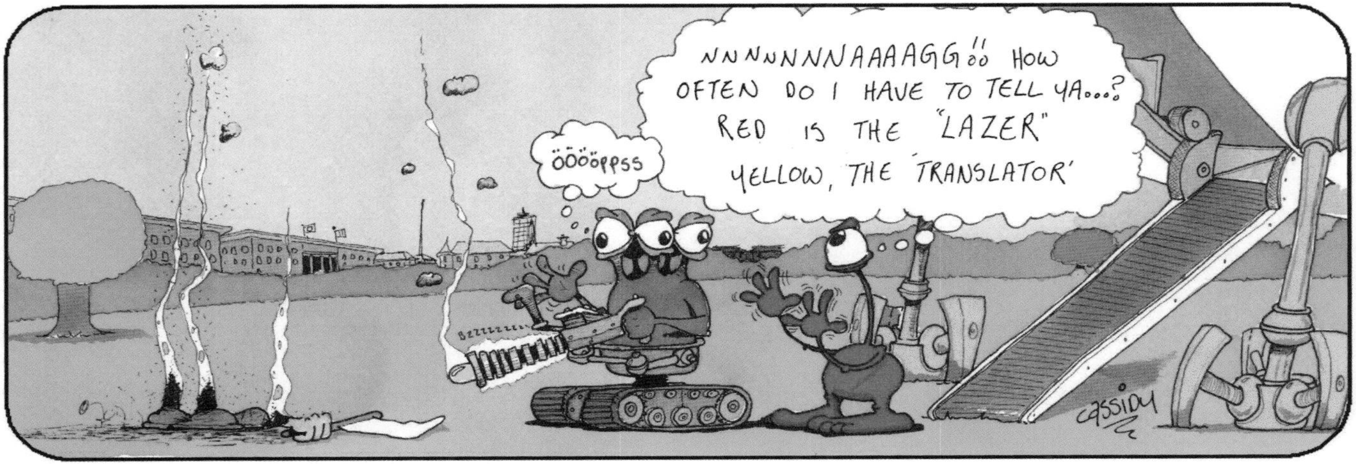
ÖÖÖÖPPSS
NNNNNNNAAAAGG!! HOW OFTEN DO I HAVE TO TELL YA...? RED IS THE "LAZER" YELLOW, THE 'TRANSLATOR'
BZZZZZZZ
CASSIDY

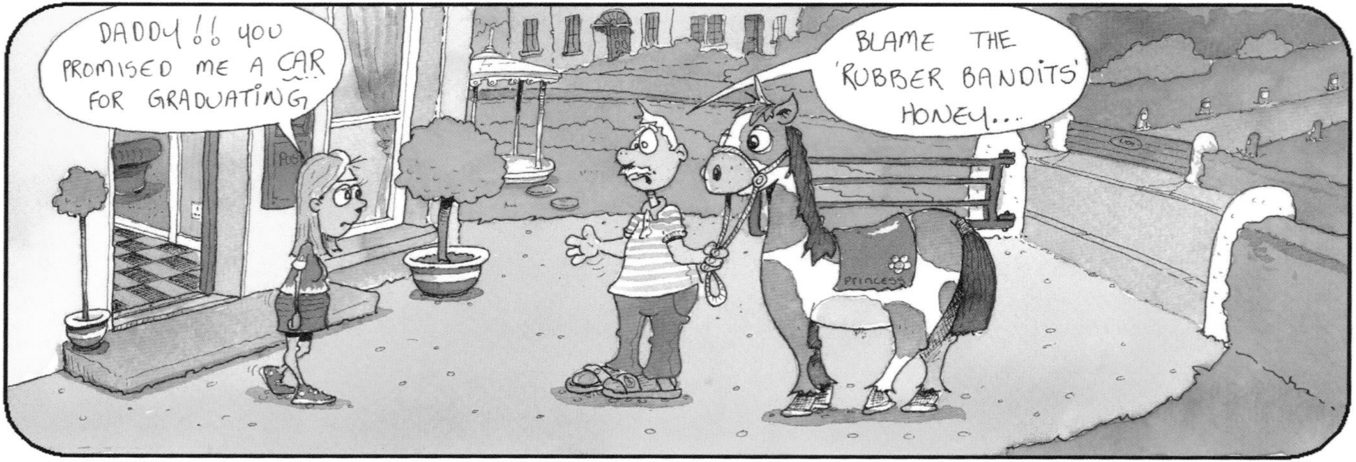
DADDY!! YOU PROMISED ME A CAR FOR GRADUATING
BLAME THE 'RUBBER BANDITS' HONEY...
PRINCESS

Dublin Daze

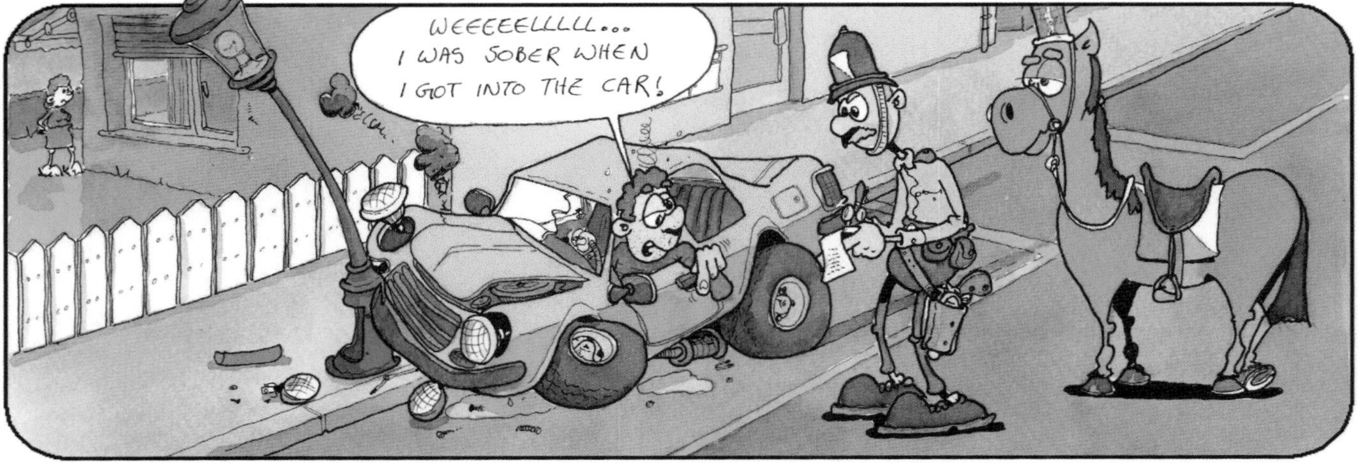
WEEEEELLLLL...
I WAS SOBER WHEN
I GOT INTO THE CAR!

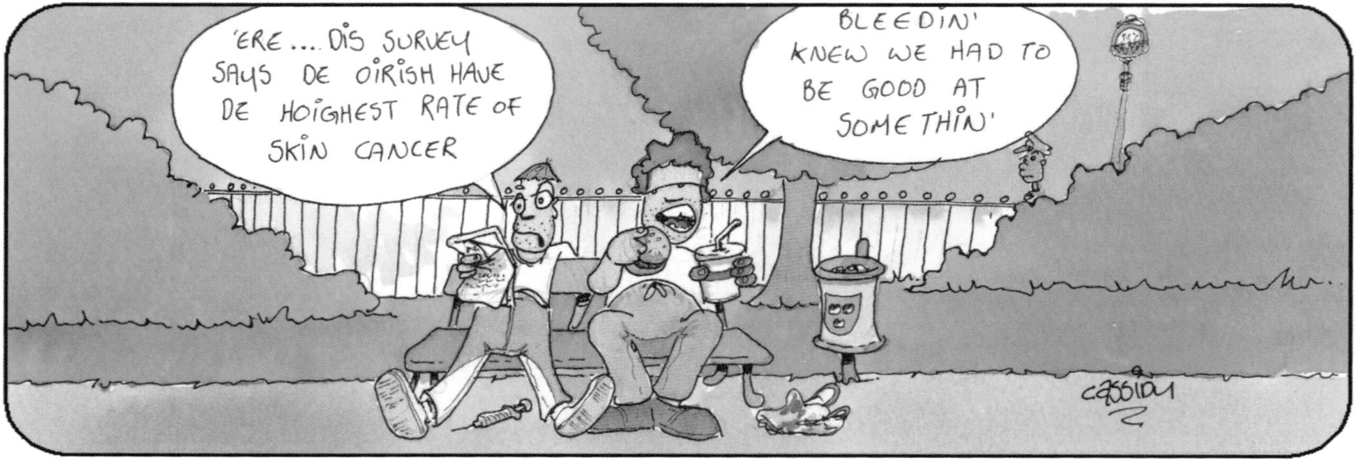
'ERE.... DIS SURVEY SAYS DE OIRISH HAVE DE HOIGHEST RATE OF SKIN CANCER
BLEEDIN' KNEW WE HAD TO BE GOOD AT SOMETHIN'
CASSIDY

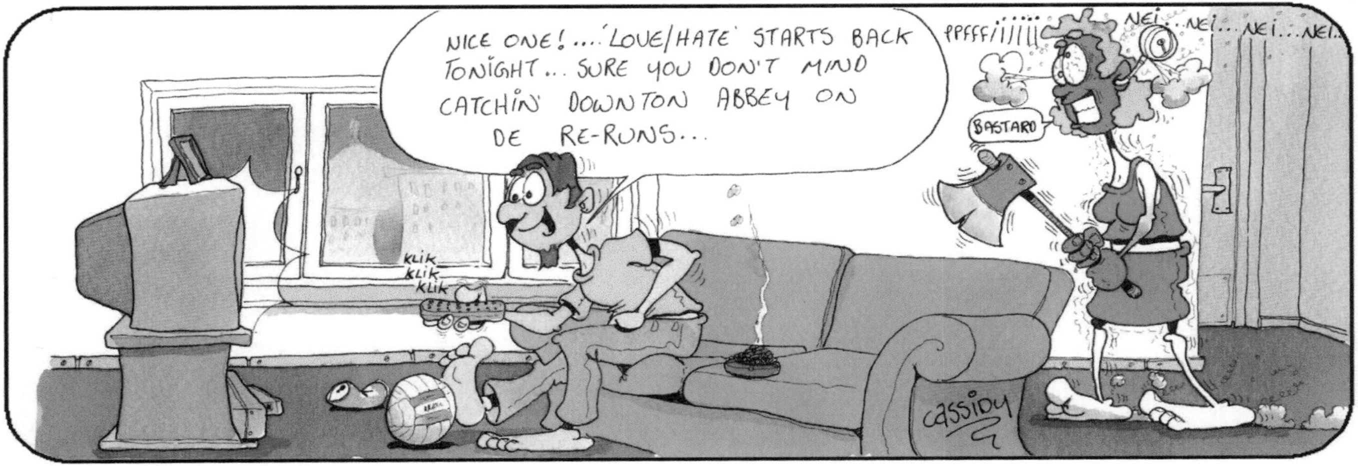
NICE ONE!....'LOVE/HATE' STARTS BACK TONIGHT... SURE YOU DON'T MIND CATCHIN' DOWNTON ABBEY ON DE RE-RUNS...
KLIK
KLIK
KLIK
PPFFF/!/!!!
NEI...NEI...NEI...NEI...
BASTARD
CASSIDY

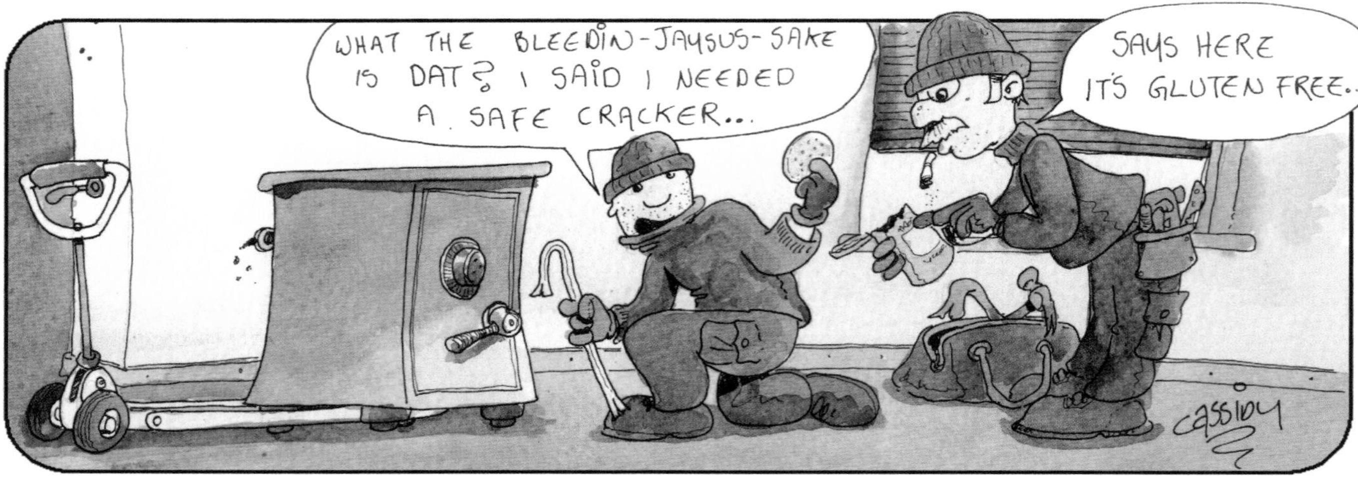
WHAT THE BLEEDIN-JAYSUS-SAKE IS DAT? I SAID I NEEDED A SAFE CRACKER...
SAYS HERE IT'S GLUTEN FREE..
CASSIDY

Dublin Daze

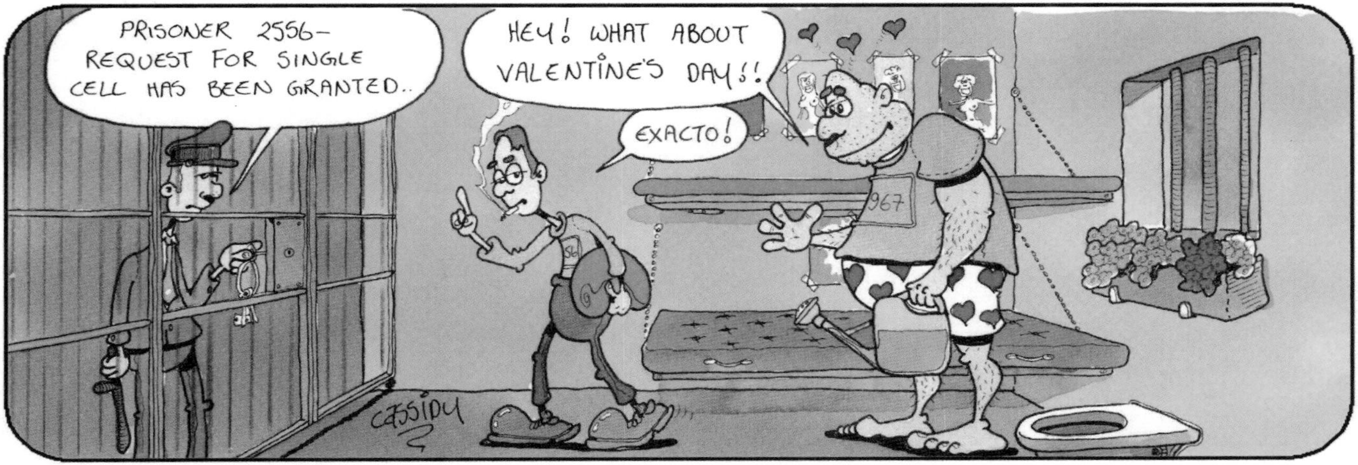
PRISONER 2556-
REQUEST FOR SINGLE
CELL HAS BEEN GRANTED..
HEY! WHAT ABOUT
VALENTINE'S DAY!!
EXACTO!
967
CASSIDY

HEY BETTY, THEM MAYANS ARE AT IT AGAIN.... THE WORLD'S TO END TOMORROW, LUNCHTIME
TYPICAL!! I'VE JUST WASHED DE FECKIN' WINDOWS..
CASSIDY

Dublin Daze

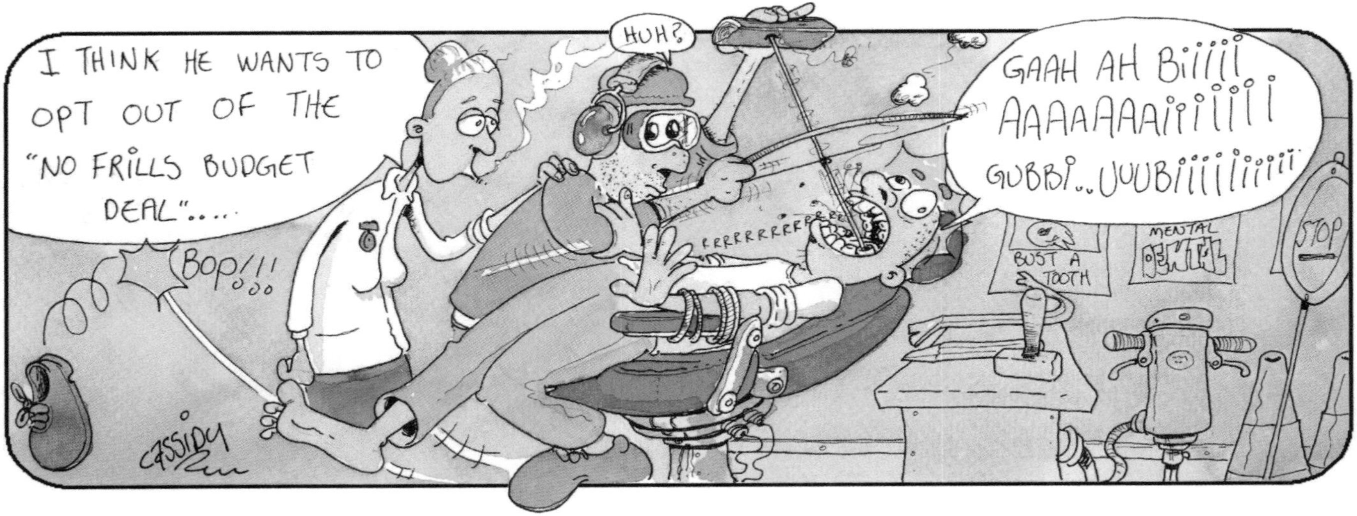
I THINK HE WANTS TO OPT OUT OF THE "NO FRILLS BUDGET DEAL"....
HUH?
GAAH AH Biiiii AAAAAAAiiiiiii GUBBi..UUUBiiiiiiiiii
RRRRRRRRRRRRRR
Bop!!!
BUST A TOOTH
MENTAL DENTAL
STOP
CASSIDY

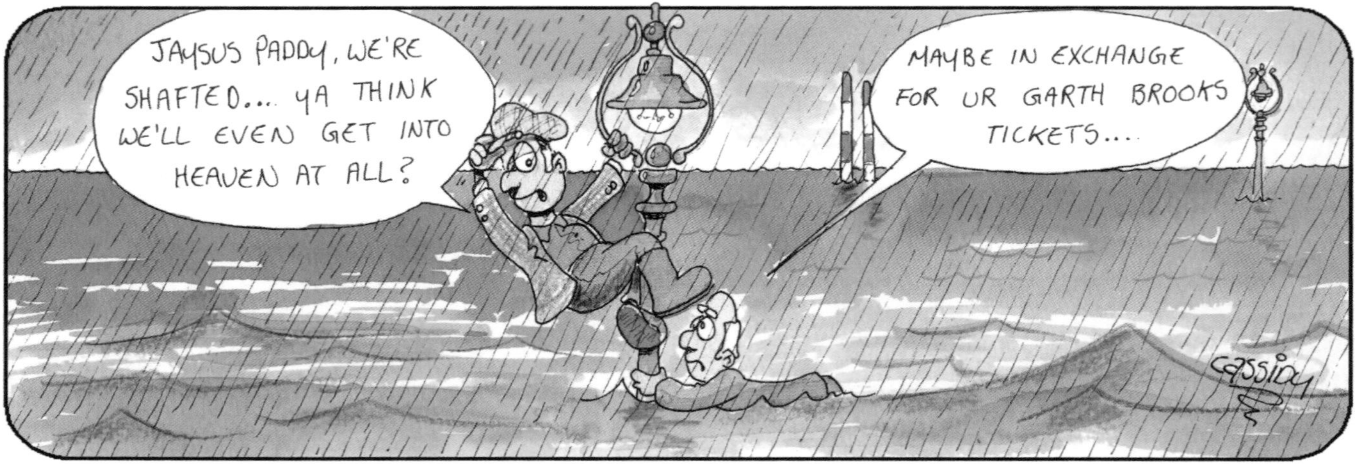
JAYSUS PADDY, WE'RE SHAFTED.... YA THINK WE'LL EVEN GET INTO HEAVEN AT ALL?
MAYBE IN EXCHANGE FOR UR GARTH BROOKS TICKETS...
cassidy

Dublin Daze

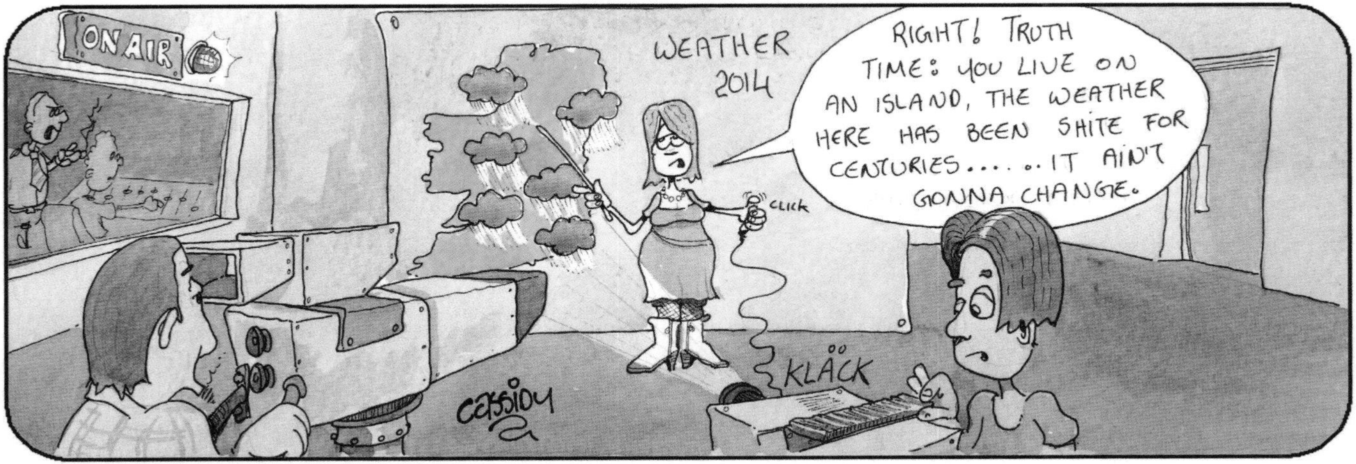
ON AIR
WEATHER 2014
RIGHT! TRUTH TIME: YOU LIVE ON AN ISLAND, THE WEATHER HERE HAS BEEN SHITE FOR CENTURIES......IT AIN'T GONNA CHANGE.
CLICK
KLÄCK
CASSIDY

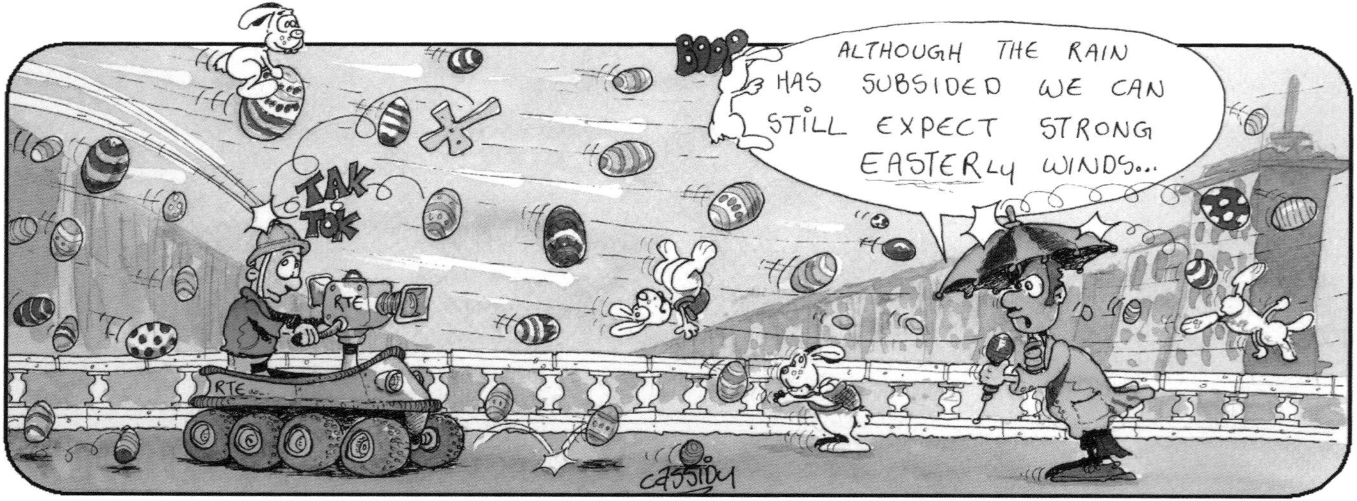
BOOP
ALTHOUGH THE RAIN HAS SUBSIDED WE CAN STILL EXPECT STRONG EASTERLy WINDS...
TAK TOK
RTE
RTE
CASSIDY

Dublin Daze

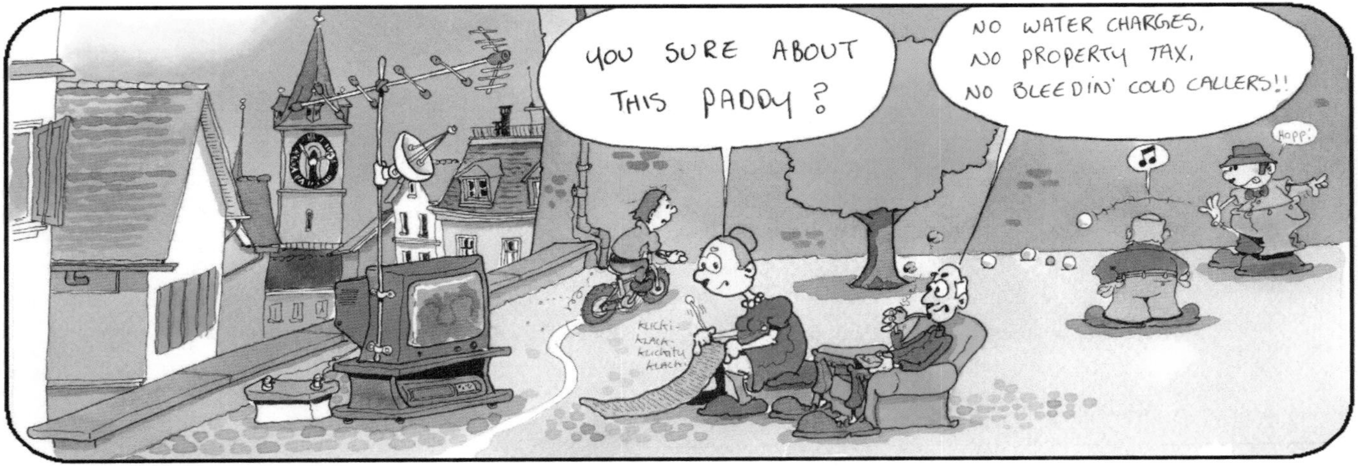
YOU SURE ABOUT THIS PADDY?
NO WATER CHARGES, NO PROPERTY TAX, NO BLEEDIN' COLD CALLERS!!
KLICKI-KLACK-KLICKITY KLACK-
HOPP!

AH JAYSUS.... THIS 'HELL' MALARKEY DOESN'T SEEM TOO BAD AT ALL... NO PITS OF DARKNESS, LAKES OF FIRE OR GNASHING OF TEETH
HAVE YOU SEEN THE WATER-RATES?
CASSIDY

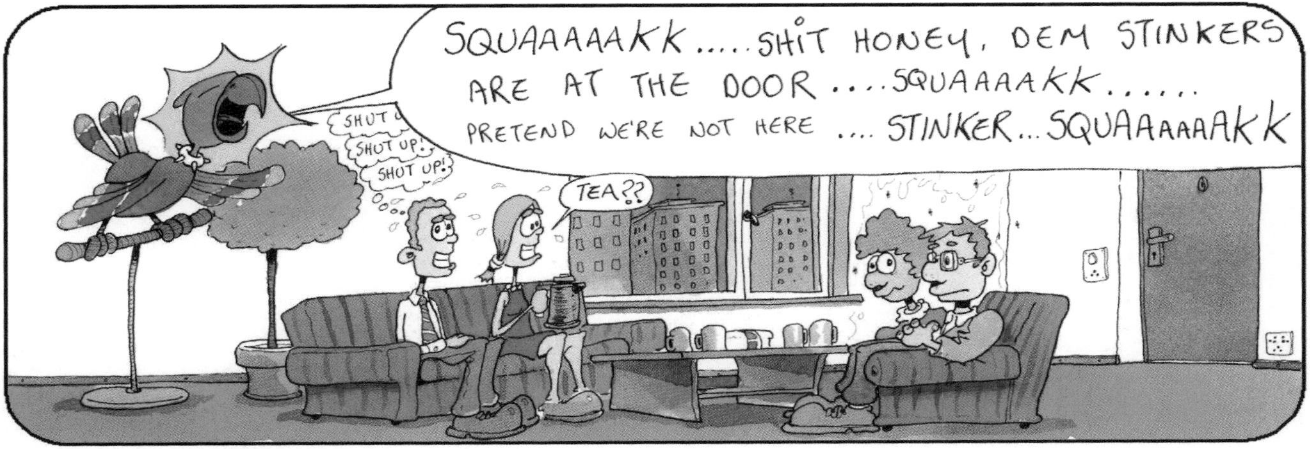
SQUAAAAAKK.....SHIT HONEY, DEM STINKERS ARE AT THE DOOR....SQUAAAAKK...... PRETEND WE'RE NOT HERE ....STINKER...SQUAAAAAAKK
SHUT UP!
SHUT UP!
TEA??

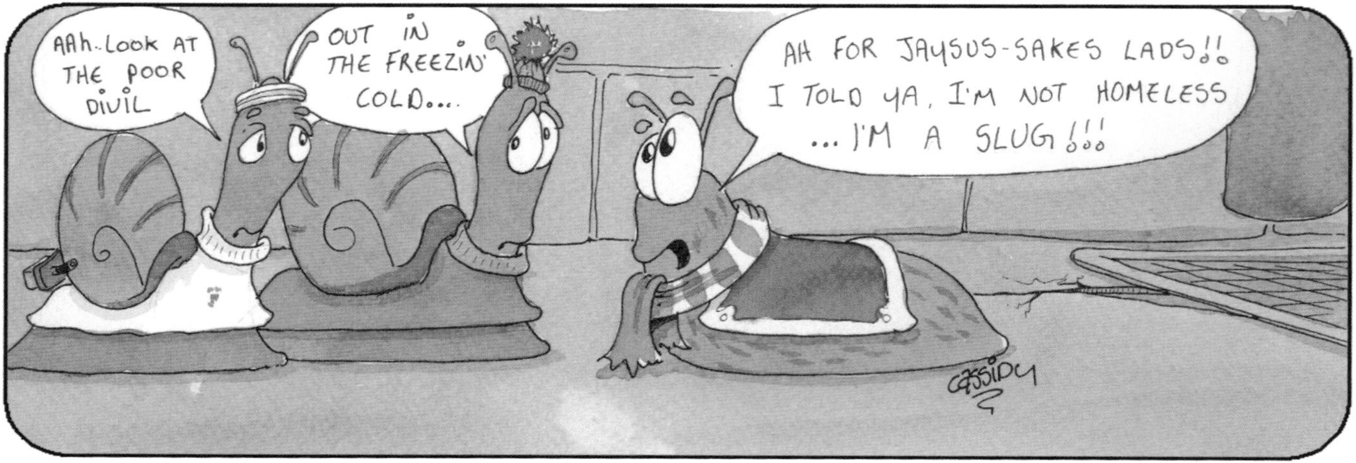
AAh..LOOK AT THE POOR DIVIL
OUT IN THE FREEZIN' COLD....
AH FOR JAYSUS-SAKES LADS!! I TOLD YA, I'M NOT HOMELESS ...I'M A SLUG!!!
CASSIDY

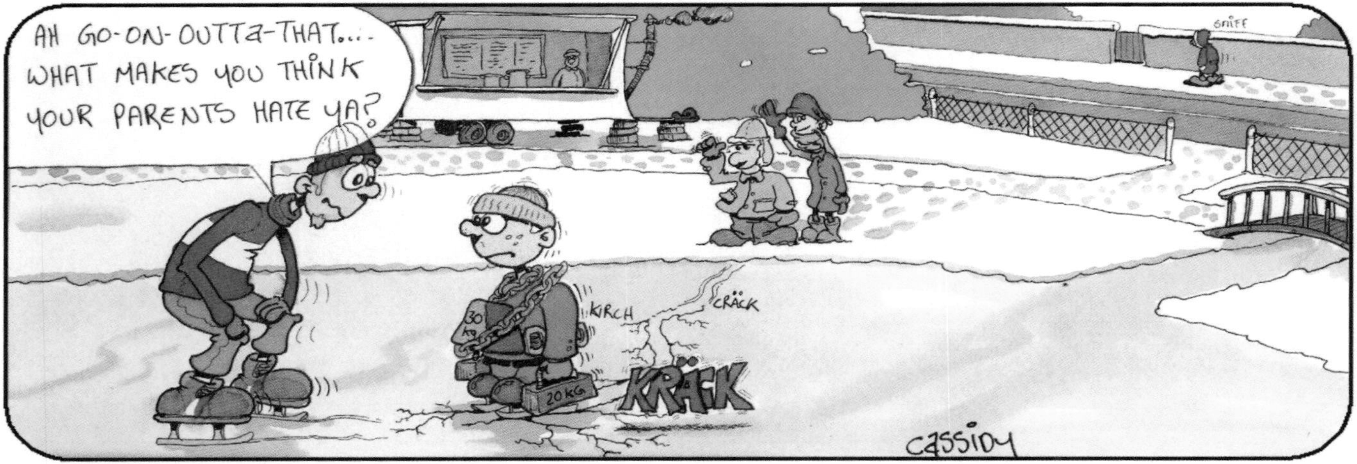
AH GO-ON-OUTTA-THAT....
WHAT MAKES YOU THINK
YOUR PARENTS HATE YA?
SNIFF
KIRCH
CRÄCK
KRÄCK
30 kg
20 KG
CASSIDY

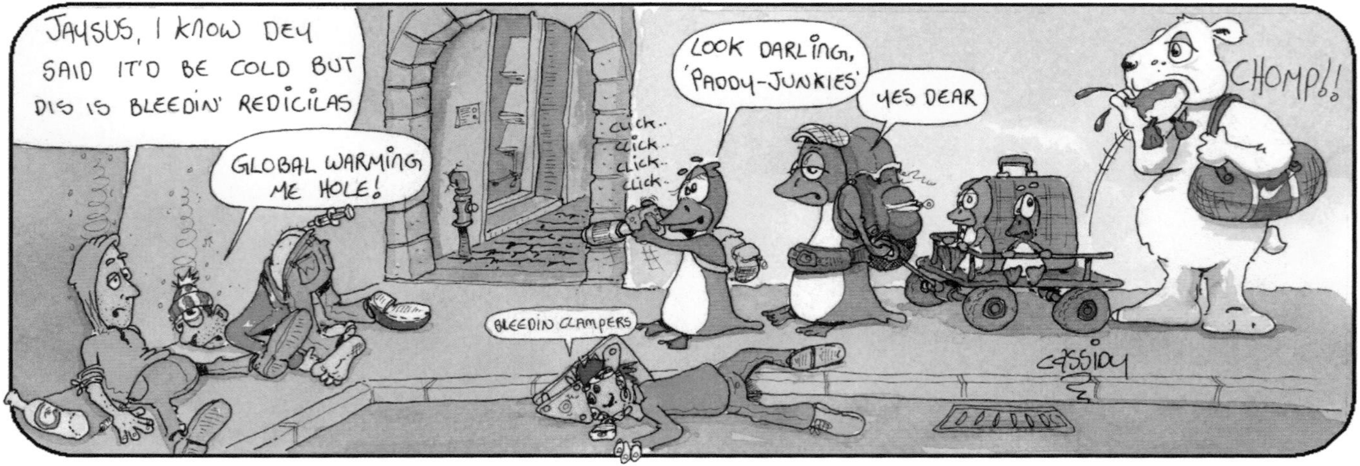
JAYSUS, I KNOW DEY SAID IT'D BE COLD BUT DIS IS BLEEDIN' REDICILAS
GLOBAL WARMING ME HOLE!
CLICK.. CLICK.. CLICK.. CLICK..
LOOK DARLING, 'PADDY-JUNKIES'
YES DEAR
CHOMP!!
BLEEDIN CLAMPERS
CASSIDY

Dublin Daze

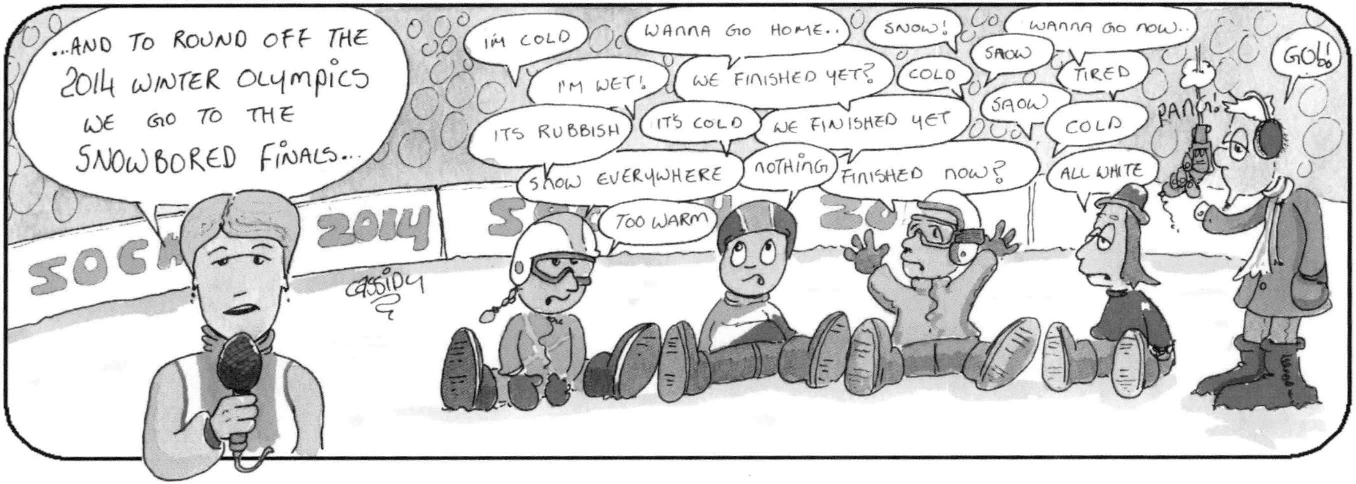
...AND TO ROUND OFF THE 2014 WINTER OLYMPICS WE GO TO THE SNOWBORED FINALS...
SOCHI
2014
I'M COLD
WANNA GO HOME..
SNOW!
WANNA GO NOW..
I'M WET!
WE FINISHED YET?
COLD
SNOW
TIRED
SNOW
ITS RUBBISH
IT'S COLD
WE FINISHED YET
COLD
SNOW EVERYWHERE
NOTHING
FINISHED NOW?
ALL WHITE
TOO WARM
PANG!
GO!!
CASSIDY

THE END

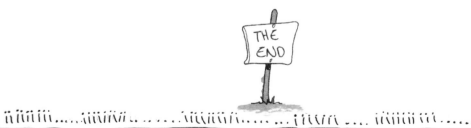

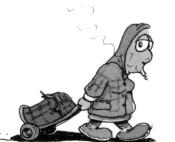

TO BE
CONTINUED

Tom S Cassidy was born and raised in the coastal village of Malahide.

Having sketched, doodled and scribbled his way through life, he has finally settled in Raheny, Dublin where he can be seen running in circles on a regular basis.

His inability to separate his cartoon world from the real world is somewhat embarrassing and bemusing for his four children, partner, family and Penny the guinea-pig, who watches him from above.

VOLUME 2.

Made in the USA
Charleston, SC
13 November 2014